How to pee in turbulence without getting your shoes wet:
and other lessons I've learned

By

Timo David

HOW TO PEE IN TURBULENCE WITHOUT GETTING YOUR SHOES WET

First edition. February 21, 2024.

Copyright © 2024 Timo David.

ISBN: 979-8224027682

Written by Timo David.

This book is filled with the thoughts, feelings and rants I've acquired in my years of living. In my 19 years as a Flight Attendant, I've learned a few things and have been annoyed by many more. Some of them may change your life. Some of them may make you laugh. Some of them may cause you to think I need professional help. I am not responsible for any lessons you have chosen to follow that have not turned out well. Think of me as Yoda but if you got Yoda on a foreign online shopping website with low quality products. Not as good or helpful as the original but still helpful, nonetheless. These lessons are in no particular order so don't assume #4 is way more important than #76. Good luck and may God have mercy on your soul if you choose to follow any of my lessons. If you bought this book expecting some awesome stories or tales of exotic layovers, you will be disappointed. I have been a regional flight attendant for 19 years. We don't fly anywhere exotic, and I have not had a ton of crazy adventures. The book started as rules for living and travel tips and became a collection of random thoughts on various issues. This is not a paper for school, so I don't care that some paragraphs go too long. I reviewed it for grammatical errors so if some still slid through, I apologize. I am not expecting anyone to agree with me on everything. However, if for some reason you find something overly offensive, please know this. The intent of this book is to make people laugh. There was no maliciousness in my writing. Also, I already have your money and no refunds are given.

The words, thoughts and ideas are mine alone and do not represent anyone I have been associated with, related to, or employed by. They do not represent any airline, or any other company associated with the airline industry. They are not endorsed by anything associated with flying including airlines, birds, other flying animals, or the ghosts of the Wright Brothers. Many of the stories are meant as humor and are not to be taken seriously. In the event I may have forgotten or misremembered the exact facts about anything that has occurred this is to state that the intent was not malicious. Some events may have been enhanced for comedic effect. I have realized there are more life lessons in here than travel ones so that's an added bonus or not.

#1

Trust Your Gut

In life you will have situations where you feel in your gut that you should do something. Do it!! Trust your instincts, most often they are telling you to make the right decision. I have had 3 memorable instances where my gut told me to do something. In 2 of them I followed my gut and ultimately my gut was proven correct. In the other situation I didn't trust my gut and I wished I had. In trusting my gut, I got to say goodbye to my grandmother before she passed away. My wife got to spend a last holiday and a week with her father before he unexpectedly passed away. The situation where I did not follow my gut, I missed the chance to see my grandfather one last time. So, listen to your gut, it might be telling you to do something that will change your life. It may save you from living with regret from not listening.

#2

Go With Mom To Church

We have become a society that no longer places a high value on religion. Church attendance no longer has the priority in our lives that it once did. Many of us have parents or grandparents who still attend church regularly. Some of them ask you to attend with them. Do it! Going to church won't make you a convert but it will mean a lot to the one you love. Do not allow the humans that have brought shame to religion take away from the fact that at the end of the day the rules God has laid out if followed make the world a better place. Time is our most valuable resource. If you give an hour a week to the people you love, it will be the best investment of that resource.

#3

Listen In Groups

In a group setting many outgoing people take the lead. This is especially true in group projects. The shy or introverted people do not have the opportunity to have their ideas heard. Often, they have really good ideas but are drowned out by the extroverts or people who tend to take control of the conversation. If you are one of those people, sit back and listen to others share their opinions. If the shy people are not forthright with their thoughts, take a moment and ask them their opinions or if they had something to add. A lot of times they are just waiting for the moment to say something, but their shyness wins out. This is a win for you, in that you are conscious of your own behavior, and you can learn something new. This is a win for the shy or introverted in that they feel included in the group and their opinion is valued. You may never know what idea or solution to a problem will be discovered by ensuring all voices and opinions have a chance to be heard.

Be A Mom's Guardian Angel

It seems now days creepy people are everywhere. The risk of child abduction is one moms, must worry about when taking their children to the store or in public. Creepy men and women following them in the store. They stare, follow and in some instances talk about their children or attempt to get the child's attention. If the mom has more than one child, they not only have to try and wrangle all of their children, but they also have to worry about their safety. If you see someone following or lurking around a mom, you can approach the mom and let her know about the creep while making eye contact with the creep. Creeps don't want to be seen, so often they will flee. If you are feeling confrontational you can call the creep out. If you do that or start approaching them, they will most likely run away. If you are in the parking lot and see a mom coming out, you can sit in your car and discreetly watch out for them. Often, they are so busy they don't see someone following them or approaching them. When they are driving away you can watch to make sure no one creepy is following them. Don't follow them as they may think you are a creep following them. Just be sure no other vehicle is following them. They may not know it, but you will have done a good deed.

#5

Say Excuse Me

It seems like no one says excuse me anymore. This is especially true on airplanes. If you are in the aisle seat and a window or middle seat passenger comes to your row, they will most likely point, grunt or say, "I'm in there". It's not difficult to say excuse me. If someone is approaching my row, I am usually looking down at my phone, so they are forced to say something to me. I am unaware they are needing to get into my row. They stand there expecting me to telepathically know they are supposed to be sitting next to me. Eventually, they will do one of the aforementioned things. Do they learn something by having to wait? Most likely not a thing. They are usually annoyed that I didn't know where they were sitting. Let's work on changing society one excuse me at a time. The next time you are on a plane and are sitting in the middle or window seat, say excuse me. You'll make the world a slightly better place and you might have to wait less time to sit down. Or you can continue to grunt and point like a caveman until your fellow passengers figure out you want to sit down.

#6

Be Nice To Special Needs People

I had the privilege of having a mom who works in special education growing up. I was exposed to more special needs people than the average person. Thankfully, we live in a society where the instances of special needs people being picked on and bullied are fewer than in the past. However, it seems a lot of times people are unsure how to interact with special needs people. In the grocery stores I frequent, many of the baggers are special needs folks. I see many times, customers either ignore them or say very little to them. They then get impatient if they go a little slower bagging their groceries. Often, they don't even thank them for bagging. You can see how much it brightens their day if you just say hello or ask how they are. I know one bagger is a huge sports fan and Star Trek fan. He and I chat about sports, and he gets really excited talking about the Georgia Bulldogs. It takes such a small amount of my time and energy and means so much to him. I know one bagger who bags really slow, but she is the best bagger I have ever encountered in all my time in grocery stores. Sometimes they aren't as high functioning as other special needs people and the most interaction you can have is giving them a smile or saying thank you. No matter how you are able to communicate, it will make a difference. No matter how small it may seem to you. It will matter to them. People behind you in line may see and be inspired to leave their comfort zone and do the same. Kindness isn't hard and it is free to give.

#7

Forgive But Don't Forget

This lesson is one of the most misunderstood rules I live by. I am told it is holding a grudge, but that is incorrect. There is a song that says scars remind us that the past is real. If you are burned by a stove, you don't hate the stove. You don't vow to never use a stove ever again. You are careful around the stove. What has happened to you makes you cautious around what hurt you. I believe in forgiveness whether that person asks for it or even deserves it. Hating that person does nothing to them and only eats you up inside. That being said, I would be cautious letting them be in a position to hurt you again. Go in, knowing the risks and deciding whether you are comfortable with a similar outcome. If you are ok with history possibly repeating itself, then give them another chance and hope for the best. If you aren't, tell them to move along. It is possible to remove them from your life and still forgive them for what they did to you.

#8

Always Tip

You see all the time on social media, servers posting pictures of rude comments or small amounts in the tip line of receipts. No matter the quality of the service, the server did give you service. Servers are humans too and as humans we sometimes have an off day. Tips are included as part of a server's pay. I am sure at most jobs, your pay isn't lowered because you didn't have a good day. Sometimes customers have unrealistic expectations or are overly needy customers. If you are one of those type of people, you need to tip extra no matter the service you receive. There are times when I have gotten terrible service. The order wasn't correct, I did not get offered a refill or get something I asked for. A lot of the times, that is the result of the server being overworked. For years, people have said if customer service people do not like low pay, they should quit. During the pandemic, customer service people took your advice and quit. So now we have short staffed restaurants and overworked servers. I have always tipped at least 10% no matter the service, and if I am by myself usually a minimum of $5. If the service is good or great, I tip even more. I tip in the hopes that if they are having a bad day. My tip will help a little, since I am sure many others are tipping very little or not at all. We don't know what is going on in the lives of the people who serve us. They may be having a personal problem, and no tips may cause their situation to get worse and their service to get even worse. This is not an excuse for giving bad service, so if your service is bad because you don't care, then shame on you. We all have received gifts we have not deserved in our lives. Give a gift to a server who might not deserve it, even if you never got your 2nd glass of Dr. Pepper.

#9

Don't Let Politics Divide Us

If you go on social media, you will know how your friends and relatives feel about most current affairs. If you live in the middle like most people, you will have friends on both ends of the political spectrum. They will claim the other side is the enemy and post their side's star politician. The other side is ruining America in their minds. They will make excuses for their side's politicians' sins but condemn the other. Often times the sins will be pretty similar. Passion in politics turns everyone involved into hypocrites. People unfriend those they disagree with, even if they are their friend or relative. They call each other names and the other is always an idiot. At the end of the day, they would rather be loyal to someone in DC who doesn't care about them, than someone they've known for years. Politicians are basically the same. Both parties use 2-3 issues to rile up their side while getting very little accomplished. A politician's number one priority is to get reelected. It is not to care about the people they claim to serve. They use you to raise money to help fight the other side. Instead of letting a few issues divide us, find out where you agree. Don't let people who want to keep their job, rob you of friendship and family. When tragedy strikes, you don't see people asking the people they help their politics. We will never agree on everything. Let what we agree on unite us and not let the other things divide us.

#10

Accept Religious Blessings From Strangers

I have known many people who get upset when a stranger says they will pray for them or wishes them some sort of religious blessing. Most of the time the religious sentiment comes from Christians, but I have experienced people from other religions bestow their religion's blessings to me. It seems like a lot of people get offended, when all the person is doing is wishing them well. You aren't converting to their religion. The thing to do is say thank you and be happy that they wished you something positive, whether you not you agree with their beliefs. I have told people I know who have gotten upset. I would rather have someone wish positivity from a religion I don't believe in, than spread negativity from a religion I do. Next time someone gives you a religious blessing or says they will pray for you, smile and say thank you.

#11

Don't be Mad When People Judge Your Appearance

Tattoos and piercings are the norm now for a lot of the population. However, there are some people who for whatever reason do not like that look. That's their preference and if they are a business owner that is ok if your look doesn't fit what they want for their business image. You are not a victim if someone doesn't hire you because of your tattoos or piercings. You chose to look that way and sometimes our choices have consequences. It is not the same as not being hired because of the color of your skin which is illegal, and also not a choice. Someone didn't just decide to go become another race while going through a phase in college or wanting to try something new. You cannot compare the two things. I am sure you are probably qualified for many jobs that you apply for and would do an amazing job for the companies you applied with. Stop crying that they didn't like your face tattoo and lip piercing and find places that do embrace the individuality you chose. If you can't find a business that embraces you, then create a business in that industry that does. You chose your appearance to not conform to everyone else's standards. Stop being a hypocrite and expecting others to conform to yours.

#12

Look Your Enemy In The Eyes

A large portion of the population seeks to avoid confrontation. When you have an enemy or a bully, they know this. They know they can intimidate you. That is why no matter how uncomfortable or afraid you are of them, or how hard the situation is, you must look them in the eye. It takes away their power. You may still feel afraid but the boldness you show will intimidate them. I have a person who has used their position professionally to attempt to intimidate me. However, all their intimidation has been from phone calls, emails and publicly lying about me. In a recent professional setting, they had to come greet a table I was sitting at. I attempted to look them straight in the eye. They noticed this and refused to look at me. They would look to my left or my right but would not look directly at me. The intimidator became the intimidated. Be bold and reclaim the power. Stare them down and show them you aren't afraid.

#13

The Key To Any Successful Relationship Are Headphones

I once was forced to attend a couple's wedding shower. My feelings on those will be addressed in another lesson. We all had to play games and write down advice for the married couple. One of the questions was, "what do you need for a happy marriage?" My answer was headphones. They collected everyone's responses and then read them aloud. There was the usual "don't go to bed angry". That kind of fluffy junk. The stuff that sounds great in theory but is not practical or ever actually works. They came to mine and read, "headphones?". Everyone was puzzled. I then explained why. Often at night I am attempting to watch tv. As she will confirm, it is never anything my wife wants to watch. She will lay on her side of the bed and watch TikToks, which interfere with my ability to hear whatever is on the television. I then have to turn up the volume to hear. She will then be unable to hear her videos. If she would wear headphones this would not be an issue. Sometimes I listen to music which she does not want to hear. Headphones allow me to enjoy music without disturbing her. Without headphones, audio anarchy prevails. Save your relationship and your hearing. Get each other a pair of headphones.

#14

Don't Stand Up In Row 45 When The Plane Parks

It never fails, as soon as the plane parks at the gate, everyone jumps up like a jack in the box. The biggest offenders seem to be the ones seated in the very back of the plane in rows 30 and higher. Or to put it more accurately, roughly behind 150-200 people. They jump up, open the overhead bins and hurriedly grab their luggage. Often, they push people out of the way or drop luggage on people's heads. I was once a victim as a passenger on a DC-9, of a suitcase dropped on my head. They mumbled an apology, but I was in pain and furious. Don't be that person. There is no need to rush. You probably have 10 minutes until it'll be your turn to get off the plane. If you are worried about your connection, the odds are you are probably going to miss it anyways. I have heard people frantic they only have 7 minutes to catch their flight. The harsh reality is your seat was dropped 8 minutes ago and the door of the jetbridge closed 3 minutes ago. Even if those things hadn't happened, unless you are Usain Bolt it is impossible to make a connection that close unless it was the gate next door. Once you hear the seat belt sign turn off, just unbuckle, remain seated and relax for the next 7-10 minutes. You aren't going anywhere so there's no need to stand up.

#15

Plan For The Unexpected

In life and especially in traveling, the unexpected happens. It is good to prepare for the unexpected. When I was a new Flight Attendant, I would plan to eat between flights but thanks to delays I wouldn't have time. Sometimes I would plan to eat near the hotel, and we would end up staying in an office park with no food nearby. I have learned to carry food with me, so I don't end up missing lunch or dinner. Sometimes I need the food and am thankful to have it and other times I am thankful to be prepared. I live in Atlanta and a considerable distance from the airport. I live 40 miles away, which can take between 40 minutes and 3 hours. When I was based in NYC, it would often take me less time to fly from NYC to Atlanta than it would to drive 40 miles. I always give myself a 30-45 buffer, in case one of the usual traffic issues pops up. Which they always seem to do. I always pack an extra change of clothes in case I am stranded an extra day on a trip or have some sort of wardrobe issue that necessitates a change. There is a never-ending list of scenarios where you could need something whether it is a tangible item or extra time. Think of your day and possible problems than could arise. Then plan how you will mitigate the effects of those problems. You might need your plans, but you will be prepared in case you do.

#16

Go To The Bathroom In The Terminal!!!

One of Flight Attendants' biggest pet peeves are passengers who rush to board the flight first and then run to the bathroom. The reason is that often it involves a Flight Attendant having to move out of the way and remain in other passengers' way until you get out of the lavatory. Then once they get out of the lavatory, many times the passenger will stand there in the way staring at all the passengers coming towards them. It means they will have to attempt to swim upstream to get to their seat. Many will ask if they can just wait to go back. Unfortunately, that is not very feasible on many aircrafts because it involves both the passenger and the Flight Attendant being in other passengers' way while they board. The Flight Attendant will tell the passenger they need to return to their seat and a lot of times the passenger will get mad. Even though it is a problem of their creation. Besides the inconvenience in boarding, the passengers also sometimes feel the need to leave a nasty smelling present from their airport burrito lunch. Our jumpseats are right by the lavatory, so we get stuck smelling your poor choice in dining all the way from the gate until 10,000 feet. If it's a busy airport like La Guardia it could be an hour, or more that we are forced to hold in our urge to vomit. I almost never say anything because if you gotta go, you gotta go. Your poor planning annoys me, but I don't want you peeing or pooping your pants. Once an older lady came back and pointed at the door behind me. I think that annoys me almost as much as them going to the bathroom. You are not a chimpanzee learning to communicate. Use your words, as we often tell toddlers. She then says, "they never give us any time to use the restroom before the flight". I already being annoyed say, "we are delayed 35 minutes. There was plenty of time." She then says, "the restrooms are so far away". I reply, "the restroom is directly across from this gate." Befuddled at my response, she is at a loss for words. Finally, she says, "well can I go?" I'm like yes you may. Next time you are on a flight go to the bathroom before you board. Obviously, if the connection time is tight and it's a choice between making your flight and going to the bathroom. Board the flight and go on the aircraft. Just don't be the first person on the plane and rush to the lavatory. Your Flight

Attendants and your fellow passengers whose way you would be in will be glad you did.

#17

Give Your Wife The Upgrade

I have seen so many times where a couple that is traveling together only one of them gets an upgrade to first class. Almost every time, the man takes the upgrade and sends the woman to coach. Many times, she has to go back to coach with children in tow. Sometimes the husband will decline the upgrade and sit with his family. I commend him for that. However, instead of "sacrificing" to sit with your family you should take the upgrade and give your wife a break by giving her the upgraded seat. Let her enjoy the more comfortable seat. Let her have a break from the kids and a glass or two of wine. You'll be fine by yourself with the kids for an hour or two. If you aren't, then you need to appreciate your wife even more. If you are traveling without children, then let her have upgrade as well instead of being selfish. She most likely isn't your level of status as she doesn't fly as often as you. She doesn't get the upgrade opportunities that you get. Don't be selfish. Let her have the upgrade. Don't be like a former NFL Quarterback who took the upgrade and sent his wife to coach.

#18

It's Ok To Say No To Something Free

Sometimes it is ok to turn down something that is free. If you are sitting in first class, you are not obligated to have alcohol just because it is free. If you wouldn't normally drink a Jack and Coke at 5:00 am you don't need to have one just because it is free on the airplane. If you are offered a predeparture drink it is ok to say no. Often boarding is going slow, and the Flight Attendants are concerned with getting the flight out on time. If they serve you a drink that will hold up boarding and make it more challenging to depart on time. While they want to be able serve you a predeparture drink if the flight departs late, they will get in trouble. More often than not, they will have to take it back from you before you finish it. You will have plenty of time to enjoy a drink in the air. The same can be said for drinks and snacks in the air. If the flight is experiencing turbulence or the flight is very short, you can say no thank you. The Flight Attendant is trying to serve as quickly as possible while trying to avoid injury. They don't need to get hurt because you couldn't go on a 43 minute flight without coffee. Buy a coffee before you leave or when you get there. Someone once waited 6 hours to eat on a delayed flight because the breakfast was free. There is no need to wait that long to eat cheerios because they are free. We won't be offended if you say no thanks. It may even decrease your carbon footprint. I have no idea how, but it may or may not. Just err on the side of caution and say no thank you. This is not to discourage you from having drinks or snacks at all but to let you know that sometimes for the sake of safety saying no thanks is the best way you can help us.

#19

Book Non-Stop Flights

Airline passengers are always looking to save a few dollars. I have 19 years of airline experience to back me up on this when I say, DON'T!! Connections exponentially increase the chance something may go wrong. You may miss your connection, or your luggage may not make the connection. I personally had to fly on the luxurious Concorde with blood-stained jeans and just a backpack because I booked a connection. I have seen many heartbroken travelers who have had their vacations or business trips interrupted by missing their connections. I had a large group of passengers on a flight miss their cruise because they booked to connect instead of going nonstop. The First Officer was trying to be empathetic to a passenger and she screamed that he ruined her vacation. The risk of ruining your vacation is not worth whatever money you save. Airlines operate with almost full planes, so the chance they can rebook you quickly is very slim. You may have to wait a day or two to get to your destination. If your connection is somewhere over an ocean, you will most likely be waiting at least a day to get to your destination. If you live in a smaller town, it may involve you having to drive to a bigger city. It is totally worth it for the decrease in odds of things going wrong. One Christmas, my parents made the mistake of booking with an airline that involved a connection. They ended up being stuck in St. Louis for 3 days in a hotel. The initial problem was due to weather, but the airline's antiquated computer system caused the several days delay. After waiting 3 days, they ended up purchasing a ticket on a competing airline. Thankfully, because of the bad publicity for the IT issues, the first airline reimbursed them for the hotel and competing airline tickets. Normally that is not the case. When traveling, sometimes the added cost or inconvenience is worth it to reduce the odds of your trip being ruined. Pay the extra money and book nonstop. You will thank me for this.

#20

Don't Drink Airplane Coffee

Whatever you do, DO NOT DRINK AIRPLANE COFFEE!!!! If you do not believe me, you are free to Google this. Airplane potable water when tested many times contains e coli bacteria. It can make you sick and be harmful to pregnant women and their babies. Every year, airplane potable water tanks are tested. They almost always test positive for e coli. The tanks are then drained until they can be flushed with disinfectant. That means the day before the tanks are tested, they are considered safe even though it is highly possible they contain bacteria at that time. Flight Attendants brew coffee before departure. It never fails that 3 to 4 passengers come on and say the coffee smells good. No, it doesn't smell good, it smells free. Midwesterners are the biggest offenders of this. If you mention that the coffee in the airport is better you get an angry response of, "I'm not paying that amount of money for coffee!!". Once a woman came on the plane and scrubbed everything on or around her seat including the ceiling. A friend came to her row to serve beverages and she ordered coffee. They looked at her and said, "you did all that work scrubbing everything down and you ordered the most likely item to have germs on my cart?' She was shocked and replied, "you mean the coffee isn't good for you?" They said, "no, it is not. Google airplane coffee". Spend the extra few bucks on airport coffee. Your body will thank you.

#21

This Isn't Open Mic Night At Giggle Plane

Before the Pandemic, this was usually only a Saturday issue. In the past, Saturday passengers were typically low yield leisure travelers. What that means is that their tickets are usually very low priced. Airlines make very little profit on those tickets. That means the clientele are usually thrifty and most of the time don't fly very often. They can be quite annoying because a lot of time they try and be funny. I would always vow to not work Saturdays. I would forget and pick up a Saturday trip. On that trip, I would curse myself for forgetting. The most common joke would be from a couple where the husband would say, "I'll have the steak and she'll have the lobster." Once is annoying enough, thousands of times over the years gets to be really annoying. A friend decided that if people were going to be telling jokes, then they would have their own amusement out of the situation. The next time someone said that they gave a really bad fake laugh. The couple loved it. The husband while laughing asked, "you haven't heard that before? He thought he was clever. My friend stopped mid fake laugh and with an annoyed tone said, "not more than a million times". Then they moved their cart to the next row, while the passengers looked shocked. Thanks to the pandemic killing off a lot of business travel, flying comedians aren't limited to just Saturdays anymore. If you feel tempted to tell Flight Attendants jokes, DON'T!!

#22

Take Out Your Headphones

This rule isn't just limited to airplanes. This is useful in all situations where someone will talk to you. It is so annoying when you are attempting to talk to someone, and they constantly yell, "what?" It doesn't matter if you turned your music off. You are still unable to hear, not to mention it is disrespectful to the other person. Just take the 2 seconds to take your headphones out. Give the person your attention, and then go back to listening to whatever you were before. This isn't something that takes much effort at all to do. All it takes is some consideration on your part.

#23

Park Further Away

If you are in a parking lot, park a further distance away from the store. There are a few reasons for this. It saves the closer spots for elderly people as well as people with children. It allows them to have a shorter distance to walk. The next reason is that it will help reduce the risk of an accident. Often if you park close, you have some sort of giant van or SUV on both sides of you. It makes it difficult for you to see, while you back out. It also makes it harder for other drivers to see you. I have seen a ton of near accidents as well as people almost getting ran over because of this. Someday, those folks may not be so lucky. I personally had an accident because of this type of situation. The driver wasn't paying attention and ran into my car. The last reason is the extra walking is good for your body. It may not be a lot of exercise, but it is still exercise. For some of us it might be the only exercise we get all day.

#24

Stand Up For Issues That Don't Affect You

This issue is one that is important but can also be misinterpreted. Standing up for something that doesn't affect you, does not mean taking over the issue from those affected. If you are affected by one of these issues, allow those who want to support you but aren't affected to help. It seems some people own an issue and get upset people want to support them. As if by accepting help, it somehow dilutes the power of the issue. If you see someone committing any type of discrimination or harassment, call it out. Let the victim know that you have their back and let the perpetrator know they are wrong. Sometimes the perpetrator is only acting that way out of ignorance and not being malicious. By being an outside observer with no emotions attached to the issue, you can explain to them how they are wrong. If it was intentional, you can let them know that you won't stand for their actions and the victim does not deserve what they did. You may not change their minds, but you will change their actions. They will know what behavior will not be tolerated.

#25

Talk To People Who Are Different Than You

In my job, I encounter people from all walks of life. A lot of them are different races, genders, orientations, political beliefs or the most offensive of all, different sports team loyalties. Most of the time, we probably wouldn't be hanging out in similar social settings. However, the airplane brings everyone together. You have a lot of time on flights, so if you are sitting next to them, strike up a conversation. Most of the time, you will only learn random things about a person. However, many times you can learn things from a different point of view that may change how you think about an issue. Since an issue affects you differently, you may not know a different point of view. Or maybe you might just learn about that person's story. Either way, that person will feel valued that you took the time to listen to them.

#26

Agree To Disagree

Thanks to social media, we are able to share our opinions on everything. That in turn has caused a lot of fighting and name calling. Some people will unfriend or block people simply for having a different point of view. It causes some people to get keyboard courage and say things to people they would not say to their face. They may engage in an argument with someone on a post. Then their friends, who weren't part of the argument join in and pile on the person with whom their friend disagreed. We will never agree on everything. We don't know why people feel some ways about issues that are different than how we feel. That doesn't make them bad people or an idiot. You don't need to insult them for their beliefs. You don't need to unfriend them. It is ok to disagree. Be the better person and say you disagree and let them know that it's ok to agree to disagree. A good rule to follow when posting, is if you said this to their face, could it upset them enough to punch you. If the answer is yes, then you don't need to say it. Don't be a keyboard coward. The same goes for in-person disagreements. While they seem to occur less often, they do still happen. Don't scream or name call. Understand that you will never change anyone's mind by yelling or name calling. Take a minute and walk away, to let the situation calm down. Then, say that you are not going to discuss the matter anymore, and that you will have to agree to disagree.

#27

Never Ever Ever Wear Crocs

This one doesn't really need an explanation. Crocs are the goofiest looking piece of footwear since moon boots in the 80s. Don't be the person that wears them and certainly don't be the person who launches into a lengthy defense about how comfortable they are. There is one exception to this rule and most rules. If you work in a profession where you wear scrubs, you can wear Crocs. If you wear scrubs, you can pretty much break any of my rules actually. Everyone else, wear whatever you'd like on your feet, socks with sandals even but never Crocs.

#28

Don't Be Afraid To Embarrass Yourself To Make People Laugh

I have acquired few skills from 19 years as a Flight Attendant. The two skills I have acquired from being a Flight Attendant are that I can fix a stuck overhead bin latch and get bins to close that most people cannot. I can also pee during turbulence without getting my shoes wet. I was able to work the title in, pretty nifty, huh? I will cover that skill later. Those skills come in handy pretty much nowhere else in life. What I have always been able to do is make people laugh. As a kid, I would intentionally mispronounce things sometimes to make people laugh. In 11th grade Spanish class, we had to travel to the elementary school down the street and perform a play in Spanish for the kids. I was dressed in a dinosaur costume to play Dino from the Flintstones. On the way back, a few classmates dared me to skip down the sidewalk. It was next to the main street in town. As I did it, people driving by, and my classmates laughed. I have never been afraid to make a fool of myself to make people laugh. Making people laugh is one of the greatest gifts you can give someone. The world is a terrible place. That laugh won't make whatever challenges they are facing any better, but for a moment they will be able to escape them and have a moment of joy. So, act the fool and do something silly. You will never know whose day you will make better.

30

#29

Never Let Someone Else's Behavior Change Yours

The world is full of idiots. On a good day, they act like idiots and on others they act worse. Do not respond to their actions with the same level of stupidity. Some people say take the high road or say that if they go low, you go high. If you work for someone who mistreats you, don't let that change the way you work. You might be awesome at your job, and they may be holding you back from a promotion you deserve. Don't let that affect how you work. Let your behavior shame theirs. If you are in customer service and a customer is rude and yelling, take a breath and respond calmly. You don't need to escalate the situation and make things worse. It will only end up badly for you. It may be hard sometimes, but remaining who you are is the best course of action in the long run. You aren't an idiot so don't become one.

#30

Give The Same Effort To The Job You Have, As You Would To The One You Want

In life, you are bound to have crappy jobs. Jobs that you are too smart to be doing. Jobs where everyone is lazy. Jobs where you are mistreated. Jobs that you could do in your sleep. They are not your dream jobs. They are more like your nightmare. It is easy to become lazy, have a bad attitude or do a terrible job. DO NOT EVER DO THAT!! Life is full of challenges, whether you are religious and believe in God or believe in Karma. Everything is a test. If you give little effort to things, you do not deserve to tackle bigger more challenging jobs. I can honestly say that being in a job that my coworkers say I am too smart for and should do something better for 19 years, putting in effort is a challenge most days. But I do. I will not allow my situation to affect my effort. I have spent the past 10 years being denied promotion after promotion including not being selected for special assignments because of people that apparently have issues with me. I have been told by managers that they were not allowed to choose me. I will not allow the people holding me back to define my effort. I know that my character will not be changed by someone without character. One of my side jobs is a job most people think is a low level job and in some respects it is. I still give 100% effort because when I do a job, I do it to the best of my ability no matter the job. I challenge you to do the same. Be the best at whatever you are doing right now. Some people may make fun of you, but I am sure they will never rise from their position because of their effort. Don't let them drag you down with them.

#31

Your Past Does Not Make You Who You Are

In life, so many people wear the labels of their past as their identity. Alcoholic, Drug Addict, Abuse victim, the list goes on. That leaves many people feeling that they are less than or undeserving of good things. It has allowed many people to be mistreated by other people, because they see their self-worth as less. They devalue themselves based on a label. You are not a label. You are not your past. Your past has helped shape your life and how you think and feel. It is not who you are. Do not let people use your past to hurt you or silence you. This is in no way meant to diminish your past suffering or what you have endured. It means your past is in the past. You may have reminders of it, but it is no longer you. You may need to talk to someone to help you walk down the path of healing. It may be hard but at the end of the path it will be just you. Whatever burdens you started your journey with can be left along the path, as you head to healing. You are you. You are not an adjective or a label.

#32

Never Mess With Someone Who Touches Your Food

This rule really doesn't need any explanation. It surprises me how often people will berate fast food employees and waitstaff about their food. I think the majority of food workers are decent people. However, I am sure like in most jobs, there are a few people who are tired of being mistreated and behave unethically. Don't be the person that pushes them over the edge, so that they do something to your food. I mean you should be kind anyways but in this situation you have more to lose. If you are a food worker, don't let some rude Karen turn you into someone that will end up fired. They aren't worth it.

#33

Don't Mess With Someone's Significant Other

I am a more logical person by nature, so my thoughts usually gravitate towards the logical before the ethical or emotional. When you consider the risk versus the reward of cheating you see that ultimately your short term fun costs you in the long run. If you are married, you most likely will end up divorced. If your partner forgives you, they may say they forgive you, but they will never trust you. You will lose what you have, and it will cost you financially. Some people end up leaving their partner and having a relationship with the person they cheated with. A lot of times, that doesn't end up working out. It is logical to think that if someone in the relationship had cheated before they might cheat again. The person who didn't cheat on their previous partner will always have doubts. If you aren't attached, don't mess around with attached people. If you are attached, you know you shouldn't be messing around with anyone else. This is a pretty easy rule to follow.

#34

Don't Mess With People's Money

This rule applies to anyone in payroll, customer service or thieves. Don't mess with anyone's money. I have had many payroll issues over the years in jobs, and it is an unnecessary pain in the butt to get my money. It usually involves several emails and eventually I get my money. It is because of people who do not do their job properly. I have had several times where I was overcharged by companies and had to fight to get my money back. It is extremely frustrating and again it is from people who don't do their jobs. It seems in this country we lose so much money from theft as well. A lot of times that happens from credit card skimming as well as other methods. I have personally been a victim of card skimming on 3 occasions. It infuriates you when you go to your bank account and see all these transactions that you did not make. To those of you who either intentionally or through laziness steal our money, STOP!!!

#35

Don't Fart With Headphones On

Sometimes in public you are forced to hold in a fart. You are unsure if it'll be silent but deadly, a little squeaker or a thunderous roar. The bathroom it seems is always a considerable distance away. Desperately, you look for a safe place that is either isolated or has a lot of noise to muffle your butt trumpet. Sometimes you feel your tummy get a little rumbly and you are sitting amongst strangers in a public place. You are wearing headphones and whatever you are listening to blocks out the noise around you. For whatever reason, it tricks your mind into thinking you are alone. You decide to conduct a colonic symphony. You unleash not one or two but an entire concerto of farts. It is then, that the terror hits you. You realize that you are not alone as you think, and these were not silent but deadly farts. They were a thunderous roar and judging from the disapproving looks around you, everyone heard them. I have been guilty of this several times. Sometimes it hits me right then and sometimes I see the angry looks and then it dawns on me. My farts were blasted out at airport pa volume level. If that happens to you, the best course of action is to flee the area as quickly as possible. If you are in the airport like I frequently am, you hope and pray none of the audience of your intestinal concert are on your flight. The best plan of action for the future is to check for an audience before letting your farts fly.

#36

Don't Grab The First Thing Off Of The Shelf

When you are grocery shopping your natural inclination is to grab the first item on the shelf. Don't do that for a variety of reasons. The first being, if the store properly rotates products, that item is most likely the oldest and least fresh. Often times, if it is a slow-moving item, it will be significantly closer to its sell by date than the items behind it. The second reason is that a lot of times, that item has fallen on the floor. Many food items are breakable, but you are unable to see that until you open the package. No one wants to buy broken cookies or crackers. Sometimes if the floor has been wet, the packaging can also have water that has soaked in or if the floor has been recently scrubbed, floor cleaner. The last reason is that if the food item is perishable, it may have sat out unrefrigerated or unfrozen and then put back on the shelf. A lot of times, customers will have an item in their cart and decide they don't want it after all. After it has been sitting in their cart for a while thawing out, they may return it to the shelf. Or even worse, it has been sitting for an extended period of time on a shelf in another part of the store. A well-meaning store employee may return it to the shelf, not knowing that bacteria has set in, or the item may have melted inside the packaging. You may be purchasing something that may make you sick or an ice cream treat that is ruined. The next time you're in the grocery store, reach further back and don't end up with food that might be wack.

#37

Check Sell By Dates

This is a big issue in a certain department/amateur grocery store chain and a rather large grocery chain. Both chains are notorious for having out of date products on the shelves. Usually in grocery stores, the packaged produce, meat and dairy items are the ones that you have to watch out for being out of date. In these two large chains it is anything that has a sell by date. In most stores, shelf stable items are usually pretty safe because of their long shelf life and how quickly they sell. In these stores, it is usually not one individual package, it is almost an entire case full of items. I found in one of these serial offenders several bags of chips that were several months out of date. I could fill several grocery carts with the number of out-of-date products I find on a regular basis. I have found several items over the years that had gone out of date a year or more prior. How does this happen, you might ask? Well, it is mostly due to lazy shelf stockers and inattentive department managers. I was once a young lazy shelf stocker that did not rotate as I stocked. I feel semi cursed and believe that is why I always find lots of out-of-date items when I am shopping. I personally do not buy packaged produce items from either of these chains and check the dates closely on the other items. I don't want to be sued, so I won't name them but will leave you with this wisdom. Check the dates and shop at your own risk.

#38

Be Nice To The Little People

As a rule, you should be nice to everyone. However, you should be really nice to the little people in a company. The overlooked and underappreciated people. They rarely get the praise they deserve or even a thank you. Your kind words may make their day. As someone whose job is routinely belittled, I cannot tell you how much more tolerable it becomes when people genuinely thank me. No company can run without the little people who make things happen. Executives and customers seem to routinely forget that. Do not allow someone's title to dictate the respect you give them. You never know who may go from janitor today to manager tomorrow. People remember those who are mean to them, but they also remember who was kind to them. In the airline industry, baggage loaders also known as ramp agents are often looked down upon by pilots and flight attendants. Their role is essential to the success of a flight being properly loaded and pushed back for takeoff. While they are not flying the plane, without them the passengers and their luggage do not get to their destination. I always try and be nice to them and offer them something to drink. One time I had extra tickets to a football game. I was going to give them away. I asked this older ramp agent if he could use the tickets. He was so appreciative. Years later, when he would see me, he would thank me for the tickets again. You never know how your seemingly little act can positively impact someone who feels unseen.

#39

Change Diapers

This is directed at men. Changing diapers is not hard. Changing poopy diapers is not challenging either. It may not be the most wonderful thing to do, and the smell may be the worst thing you ever experience. You will survive. It may be a total blowout that involves an outfit change, and you will be cleaning off half of your child's body because it is poop covered. You can do it. For some reason men seem to think diaper changing is 95% or in some cases 100% Mom's job. That is false and completely selfish. It is totally unfair for someone who grew that little person for 9 months to be expected to continue to do everything for them. It's time for Dad to step up and do his job. Trust me, nobody wants to change a diaper. You always have the risk of getting peed or pooped on. That's why, if you do it more often, you can perfect getting it done quickly and efficiently. They always warn you about boys peeing on you while you change them. Because I became a pro at Nascar pit crew speed diaper changing, I have never been peed on. Mom will appreciate your help even if she doesn't mention it. Her friends will see you stepping up and tell Mom how awesome you are. Brownie points are always good. You can thank me after you become Super Dad and get all the perks that go along with that.

#40

Don't Be Embarrassed To Buy Tampons

This addresses one of the dumbest things men are guilty of doing. If your lady asks you to buy tampons, do it with pride. Don't be ashamed or nervous. I have never understood why men are so scared of buying tampons. What is important is buying the exact brand, type, and size they tell you to get. Don't go rogue and try to buy the cheap brand and light when she asked for Tampax Pearl Super. There is nothing to be embarrassed about. All it means is the cashier knows you have a woman in your life. You might even get a smile and a comment about how she wishes that her man would buy tampons for her. It is super easy to do, and you will get more brownie points for doing it without complaining. As men we are prone to being idiots, so we need as many brownie points as we can get. Hold that box of tampons high as you triumphantly march to the checkout. Let everyone see that you're a man who is not embarrassed to let the world know he has a woman at home. If they're super, you might want to pick up some chocolate as well. I am not going to get into the why. Just buy the good quality chocolate.

#41

Be Ready To Order

This is one of my personal pet peeves. When you are at a restaurant or on a plane, please be ready when it is your turn to order. There is nothing more annoying to the person trying to serve you than having to wait or come back to you. In restaurants, I have seen people talk and talk before looking at the menu. They make the server come back multiple times and a lot of times they are impatient when the server isn't there at the exact time, they are ready to order. Stop wasting the server's time and figure out what you are getting. Then, you can share the latest gossip without interruption. It isn't hard at all. It is called being considerate for other people's time. Time is our most precious resource. No one can ever have more of it. Respect their time and they will appreciate it.

#42

Put Your Cart Back

When you are done shopping, return your cart to the store or the cart corral. This isn't a hard task. My first job was at a grocery store pushing carts. I would find carts all over the parking lot and in surrounding parking lots. Carts left in the middle of the parking lot can roll into other cars, scratching or denting them. They block parking spots as well. Don't make more work for other people or risk damaging cars. One day it could be your car that is scratched by an abandoned cart. Do the right thing and take your cart back.

#43

Put The Divider Behind Your Groceries

This is another easy thing to do. When all of your groceries are on the checkout belt, put the divider behind them. The person behind you then knows it is ok to start putting their items on the belt. The cashier doesn't get confused and accidentally ring up the next customer's cereal box on your order. I have seen people get angry at the cashier when it is their fault for not putting the divider behind their groceries. Whenever I see a person in front of me put the divider behind their groceries, I thank them. I tell them that is my good person test. I joke that they could be an axe murderer, but in my book, they are a good person. That always makes them laugh. This is another simple thing that everyone should do. Being considerate shouldn't be such an afterthought for so many people. In the 80s and 90s, the saying was be kind rewind. We can say don't be a jerk, put the divider behind your groceries. It doesn't rhyme but gets the job done. For those of you who have no idea what be kind rewind means, it means rewinding your movie before returning it to the video store. It's like going backwards in your Netflix movie until the beginning because you were not able to simply click start over. It took a while and people would buy these machines where its only purpose was to rewind tapes at high speed. Some video stores would even fine you for not rewinding the movie before returning it. You really do not know how we suffered. Anyways, put the divider behind your groceries.

#44

Couples Showers Violate The Geneva Convention

I don't know when this became a thing, but it is one that needs to go away. The thing is couple's showers. One might think that this is some sort of romantic thing like a couple's massage but it is quite the opposite. It is basically a women's event that men are forced to attend. It is like a hostage situation/ funeral for the man. I was forced to attend one once. It wasn't as bad as a root canal as there was a good amount of food. It was all the other stuff like the games and present opening. I have never understood public present opening. It's like, "hey, let's see who we can make feel bad for giving a present that isn't as nice as Aunt Janet's." It is time consuming and then someone has to scramble to find the card to see who it was from so they can publicly thank them. You won't have to find the card for Aunt Janet's present because as she sees it opened, she will have to indulge everyone in an unnecessary story about why she bought it. You want to tell her that most people don't know her or even care why she bought it. The games and writing down advice things are dumb as well. I gave good advice for creating a happy marriage and was shamed. I am sorry that my perfectly logical advice wasn't some cliché. Marriage is what people choose to do like tattoos. You want a tattoo knock yourself out. You want to get married here's a present in exchange for dinner and cake. Don't make me suffer twice for your life choices.

Everyone Knows Why You Have A Shared Facebook Account

There are two reasons why couples have shared Facebook accounts. The first and most acceptable one is that you are old. More than likely, Carol runs the page so she can share political memes from Tucker and see pictures of the grandkids. Bob's name is just on there so everyone knows it is both of theirs, but more than likely he has never logged in or knows the password. The other reason is your relationship has trust issues. Ryan clicked like on a female coworker's vacation bikini pic or Jenny has been too chatty with an old high school boyfriend. One of them has given the other an ultimatum. The solution is the joint page so the other person can see what messages are being sent or pictures liked. "We decided to have a shared page for the relationship". There was no we in the decision. One person made the decision. I just want those of you with joint pages to know two things. Firstly, we all know. Second and most importantly the one you have trust issues with, more than likely has another Facebook account you and your friends are blocked from seeing or they have an Instagram account. In the end, your trust issues won't be solved and the rest of us will get a little amusement.

#46

Buy Your Kid A Seat On The Plane

This is an issue where common sense loses out to frugality. Children under 2 are not required to occupy their own seat on an airplane. You would not hold your child in an automobile going a fraction of the speed, but you are ok with holding them going 500 mph. A variety of things can go wrong. If the plane aborts take off or even stops suddenly while taxiing, your child can go flying and can get hurt. If you hit turbulence, your child can fly up and hit the overhead bin and get seriously hurt. If the plane makes an emergency landing or crashes, you will not be able to hold onto your child no matter how much you think you can. Your determination and will as a parent cannot defeat physics. There is also the making your fellow passengers angry reason. Typically, children a few months old sleep and are not a problem being held during the flight. However, once they reach 8 months or so they do not want to be held. It is uncomfortable and they let you and everyone else know that. That is when they cry, scream and kick. The passengers around them are disturbed and annoyed. In my 19 years as a Flight Attendant, the children in seats are more comfortable, better behaved and usually fall asleep for a good portion of the flight. Everyone around them is happier and the child is safer. So next time, buy them a seat.

Never Connect Through NYC

Never ever, ever, ever, ever, ever book a connection through Newark (EWR), JFK or La Guardia (LGA). It doesn't matter how much money you will save or how much time you will theoretically save. You are making a dangerous gamble. The NYC air space is one of the busiest air spaces in the world. If one cloud appears in the sky, all three airports typically experience delays. Since those airports are so busy, the odds of you missing your connection are very high, especially in bad weather. Also, in bad weather a lot of flights cancel. You may arrive in time to make your connection and still end up stranded. In every plane ticket's fine print there is a clause called an Act of God clause. Basically, it says due to weather the airline isn't responsible. You will not get a hotel if your flight cancels due to weather. NYC is very expensive for hotels in normal conditions and once flights cancel, the prices skyrocket. Hotels also fill up quickly. A passenger once asked me the best airport to fly into NYC to avoid delays and cancellations. I said fly into Pittsburgh and drive. He laughed and I said I was serious. Your best course of action is to avoid these airports if possible.

#48

Bring An Empty Water Bottle When You Fly

Flying dehydrates you. Water in the airport is expensive and often the bottles are not very big. Flight Attendants have a limited supply of water on board. Please don't come on the plane expecting us to use half our bottled water supply to fill your giant gallon sized water bottle. A lot of airports have special drinking fountains designed for filling water bottles. If they don't, they always have the old-fashioned drinking fountains. It may be annoying and take forever but you will save money and feel better while flying. If you care about the environment, you will be doing your part as well by using a reusable bottle.

#49

Don't Go Barefoot On Plane

I shouldn't even have to mention this but alas here we are. The floors on airplanes are the furthest thing from clean you can find. They may be lightly vacuumed several times in a day, but they are not scrubbed clean. I honestly don't know when plane floors are truly scrubbed but it is not very often. I am sure of that. The most disgusting thing is when people go into the bathroom barefoot. Almost every flight, the bathroom floors are wet. That is not water. That is pee. If you are barefoot or in socks, you are stepping in pee and sometimes poop or vomit. You may not be able to see them, but the germs are there. Sometimes the blue juice leaks out as well. It is a very hazardous liquid. I know of a Flight Attendant that received chemical burns on her feet when blue juice leaked out under her jumpseat. So, the next time you're on a plane, keep those shoes one. Your body will thank you.

#50

Don't Swear In Public

It seems that as civility in society has decreased so has appropriate behavior in public. The phrase used to be cursing like a sailor but pretty much everyone swears in public now. It's not cool, it's actually kind of trashy. Children are pretty much everywhere and do not need to hear your potty mouth. This is usually where some loudmouth responds with some claim of free speech. Yes, we do have the right to free speech, but rights come with responsibilities. You cannot yell fire in a crowded place as it will create panic. It's not hard to keep it classy. Imagine your grandma was there. I don't think she would find it appropriate to use the f word as an adjective. I'm sure that McDouble was tasty but was the f word really necessary? Once at a baseball game, these idiots in front of me were swearing. A family asked them to stop, and they continued. For some foolish reason, I decided to play hero and yell at them. They turned around and I stood up. There were 4 of them and 1 of me. I thought to myself, this may not end well for me. I went off on them for their inappropriate behavior. I am still shocked how it turned out, because they apologized to the family, turned around and sat down. If you feel the urge to swear, use Christian swears like golly and freaking. Or from the movie Rookie of the Year, "funky buttloving". Be a better person. This really isn't that hard. As someone who occasionally says a swear or three, I know it may seem tough, but it is possible. Ironically enough, I didn't start swearing until after one year attending a Christian college. My excuse was I was 18 and immature. I'm 42 now so I guess I'm still immature. I was ejected from an intermural softball game for swearing at the umpire. I thought I looked tough walking across the field after getting ejected. In reality I looked like an idiot. Don't be an idiot

#51

Realize That You Get What You Paid For

This is especially true in the airline industry. People pay the least and are surprised that things do not turn out as they thought they would. My favorite example of this was a few years ago. A pilot and I were waiting to take a flight on another airline to commute home. This low-cost airline similar to a bus service that frequently makes the news for fighting passengers had one of their passengers come over to our gate to complain to us. I informed her that we worked for neither airline but were merely looking to take a flight home. She started to complain to us about her flying bus flight being delayed and everything going wrong. I stopped her and said, "Ma'am, you paid $12 for your ticket. What did you think was going to happen?" She stopped and thought for a second. I was expecting her to yell at us. Instead, she responded. "you're right. I did this to myself". Then she walked away. Paying more won't guarantee perfection but paying less is often times your ticket to misery.

#52

Little People Don't Make The Rules

Customer service people have the hardest jobs. Often, they are required to enforce or are limited by rules they did not create. Many times, they are rules they do not even like or agree with. They may know a better solution but because of the corporate hierarchy they are required to follow the rules. In the airline industry, the biggest example of this were the masks for COVID. We did not create the rule but we were expected to enforce it. I personally did not have anyone who refused to wear a mask, but I know several people who did. I also see this every Sunday at the grocery store. They cannot sell alcohol before 12:30pm. It never fails, there is always a pile of alcohol at the registers from people who tried to purchase it before 12:30. I have seen people yell at the cashier for a law they didn't create. For some reason, angry customers decide to direct their anger and frustration at the person who has no power over the rules. This is really stupid, as they did not make the rules and do not possess the power to change them. They don't deserve your wrath. Be an adult and take it up with the people who created the rule and have the power to change it.

#53

Be Needed Not Needy

There is an old saying that the squeaky wheel gets the grease which is sometimes true. The squeaky wheel also gets replaced. In life and in the workplace, people who possess special skills or a willingness to step in and help are valued. People who constantly need help or have problems are not. We all have someone who only calls when they need something. Whether it is to call and complain about their current dilemma or they need help, their call is not usually wanted. Needy people complicate life and are an extreme annoyance. This is not referring to people who have legitimate needs like children, the elderly or the disabled. It is people who have no value in life. They do not contribute. They only take. They are leeches. They are always glad to join in on something if someone else is paying. That may be dinner, sharing a hotel room at a resort or helping themselves to someone's favorite sodas when they are over. They take and do not give. They are unneeded. The good news is if that describes you, you can change. You can stop taking and you can give. You can stop being Minnie the Moocher and be someone people want to be around. It's all up to you. I promise everyone will be glad you did.

#54

Do Laundry

One of life's mysteries that I will never understand is how difficult people make doing laundry out to be. "Laundry never ends". "There is always so much laundry. Didn't I just do laundry?" LAUNDRY IS NOT HARD!!! You do not need to wash it in a stream or use a washboard. Thanks to technology, is it one of the easiest things to do in life. Yet, it is the source of so much complaining. If you are a husband, you can earn so many brownie points by doing something so simple. I am going to give a very easy step by step process to accomplish this task. Step one, put laundry in washer. Step two, watch something on one of your favorite streaming platforms. Step three, after an episode or two is over, put laundry in dryer and more laundry in washer. Repeat step two. Then take laundry out of dryer and put into a basket. Repeat step three and then repeat step two. While watching your favorite show, fold and put away clean laundry. After a few hours of watching your favorite shows, the laundry is complete. Now accept your prize as husband of the year.

#55

Do Jobs Other People Won't

This one has two different interpretations which are both valuable advice. A lot of jobs have things that employees don't want to do. Usually there is a reason. It is either a lot of extra work or just an all-around crappy job to do. Volunteer to do them. It will show your bosses you are willing to work hard and go the extra mile. It may benefit you on your yearly review, may help get a pay raise or even get you a promotion. Companies like people who are willing to do what it takes to help the company. If it involves learning an additional skill, that also makes you more valuable than your coworkers. If layoffs happen, that will make it harder for them to make you one of the first ones to get laid off. The other interpretation is don't be too proud to make money. There are a lot of jobs many of which are service related, that people are too proud to do. I have spent 3 years delivering groceries. Most people look down on that, but I have made more money than I would have than if I used my MBA. If you have bills or a family who needs to eat, do what you need to do to make money legally. It will take checking your ego, but it is worth it. Don't starve because of your pride.

#56

Give Effort

One of the hardest things to do is anything you don't want to. It may be a job you hate. Give effort like you love it there. So many people do the bare minimum but expect maximum results. We have become a country of the half assed because it is just enough. We are all guilty of doing as little as we can get away with in one area or another. Take pride in what you do even if you hate it. Once you take pride in what you do, it may become more tolerable. Do your best. Sometimes people notice and sometimes you are doing it just for yourself. Often, people won't notice. Don't let that deter you from working hard. If you are an employer, don't abuse those people. Value their effort and don't take advantage of them. Many employers do and that discourages the rest of their workforce from doing more.

#57

Read

This may seem simple but sadly for most people it is hard. Read. Read books, magazines, news articles, and anything else you can find. We learn by reading. You may learn something unimportant but someday it may come in handy. Read the news. The world is constantly changing, and it is good to be in the know of current events. Don't read from just once source. Most news agencies have some measure of bias now days. Read from both sides of an issue. You will see how both sides distort an event for their narrative. Both sides are guilty of that. An old saying is there are three sides of an argument, yours, mine, and the truth. That seems to be so true now. Read like you can earn a free personal pan pizza from Pizza Hut like in elementary school. You will become so much more knowledgeable and a popular teammate on trivia night.

#58

Don't Be Afraid To Stand Alone

A lot of times on issues there are others who will support your views and beliefs. Sometimes you are the only one. Many times, that causes people to be quiet about their feelings and go along with the majority. They are afraid of standing up and being the target of criticism. Sometimes in arguments, people don't argue fairly and will attack the person and not the argument. When that happens, just steer them back to the argument and point out that their other statements are irrelevant. It is better to stand alone and be right than go with the flow and be wrong. In history, so many times people have chosen to be silent and bad things have happened. I'm not saying your silence will cause something bad to happen. I'm just saying your issue is not new but there have been some bad consequences from silence. Sometimes all it takes is one brave voice for others to gain theirs. Be the person who stands for their beliefs even if you sometimes have to stand alone.

#59

No Christmas Music Before Thanksgiving

Christmas music seems to be either loved or hated. There does not seem to be a middle ground. I am of the group that hates Christmas music. It's not because my extended family Christmases were never joyous and were actually kind of painful. I've repressed those feelings. It's not because it signaled the start of the eternal winter I lived through as a child growing up in Minnesota. It's because I truly do not like the songs of Christmas. I know that is sacrilegious as Christmas celebrates the birth of Christ. I can't help it. I do not like the songs. It seems like a certain red discount department chain that is the main offender of seasonal creep. Every year they put out decorations for the next season earlier and earlier. Mid-October, my local store already had 2 rows of Christmas merchandise set and they looked to be converting more rows. Enough already!! Let Halloween have its time. Thankfully the radio has not succumbed to that yet. However, many people choose to play Christmas music early. Do not be one of those people. The day after Thanksgiving is the only acceptable time to start playing Christmas music. You can wait a few more weeks. I know you can do it!!!

61

#60

Take Creepy People's Pictures

The world is full of a lot of people with bad intentions. You see them lurk or linger in stores or around people's houses. They may be looking to kidnap or abuse a child. They may be looking to rob or steal. The key to them being successful is their anonymity. Take their picture and let them see you are taking their picture. They will almost always run away. There is a rare chance they may try and confront you. Don't be afraid and tell them you are concerned about your safety. If they are innocent, they more than likely will be quiet. If you are bold and take their picture you may not only be keeping yourself safe but others around you as well. If they still commit a crime, you will at least have evidence of who they are. That will help the police catch them as well as warn others to be on the lookout for them. This also is true for suspicious vehicles that linger. Take a picture of the vehicle and especially the license plate. Take a picture of any damage or customization that can help identify it. I had a suspicious person try and get into my house. I confronted them on the video doorbell, and they left. I saw their vehicle again and ran out and took a picture of their plate. I called the police per their instructions after the first incident and relayed the license plate to them. It may seem scary, but you will never know the full impact of what you did by taking a picture. You may have prevented a crime or might help solve one.

#61

Don't Fight On Black Friday

This really shouldn't have to be said. No one should be fighting to save a few bucks on a set of sheets. But alas, every year there is some fight usually in New York and someone gets punched, stabbed or shot. It's not worth dying or going to jail for a bargain. Not to mention it makes you a tremendously terrible person. If you are smart, you will see that a lot of times the deals before Black Friday are better than the ones on Black Friday. No need to camp out or fight the crowds and the post turkey drowsiness. Once, I got a laptop a week before Black Friday for a price cheaper than the same laptop on Black Friday. One year in my younger days, I camped out to save a few hundred dollars on a laptop. I almost froze and around 3 am some people let us hang out in their tent. We felt like we were freezing to death while screaming out song lyrics to stay awake. It was an experience I will never relive again. Right before the doors opened, this family tried to jump the line and a brawl almost ensued. Don't be those people and don't be someone who values a discount more than dignity.

#62

Leave The Family At Home

If you have ever been foolish enough to go to a warehouse club store on a Saturday, you will understand my annoyance. Do not bring your whole freaking family to go shopping. Families come and walk across the width of the aisle and look like a superhero group slow motion walking in a movie. They take up the whole freaking aisle and get annoyed someone else might want to shop in the store. Let me be clear, this is not referring to young children. It's when people bring their 15yr old kids. All of whom seem completely clueless to their surroundings. Then when they see samples, they all line up like it's a UN food drop in a third world country. They block the aisles and are worried if they move, they might miss out on a 1/364 size slice of pizza. It's just not one inconsiderate family at a time. It's tons of them. They clog up the whole freaking store. It is enough to drive you insane. I just want to yell, "Stay Home!!" In the future, please limit your visits to 2 family members. Your teens don't care that 56lb boxes of protein bars are on sale and probably would rather be sitting at home or basically anywhere else.

#63

Don't Hold Grocery Store Reunions

This may sound like the last one, but it is completely different. It seems like women are mostly the guilty parties, but men are guilty as well. This may be due to the majority of grocery shoppers being women. Men seem to be a little more situationally aware when they are creating chaos. It all starts when Carol decides to go grocery shopping. She is in the back aisle by the milk and sees Nancy. They haven't seen each other in a bit so they start chatting. They stand in the middle of one of the main aisles in the store. They are completely clueless that they are in the way of almost every shopper, nor do they care. Occasionally, someone will say excuse me. They will get slightly annoyed that they have to move, even though they are the problem. It will take a minimum of 4 fellow shoppers to say excuse me before they get the hint. They won't realize they are the problem and will say something passive aggressive about everyone else. During the pandemic, we were told to stay home to keep the sick and elderly safe. The thing that irritated me the most, was that grocery stores were full of the elderly not social distancing. They were all standing close together talking for a long time. We will never know if this mattered or not but at the time it was completely the opposite of what we were told was safe. I was like, "grandma, I can't eat inside any restaurant to keep you safe, and you are being completely unsafe." The next time you are in a grocery store and see someone you know. Just say hi and keep it moving.

#64

Don't Argue Rules With Flight Attendants

I have been a flight attendant for 19 years. I know most of the FAA rules regarding my job. There are some obscure ones most people do not know, but the majority of the rules most of us know. It never fails, someone decides they want to argue the rules. If you are in the front row, you cannot put your bag in front of you on the floor. The response is sometimes, 'since when?" or my favorite, "they let me on the last flight". Well in the 19 years I've done this job, it's been the rule. I also don't care if they let you break the rules on the last flight. On this flight, we follow the rules are my responses. They grumble but comply. The majority of us do not want to have to enforce the rules. It would be much easier and less confrontational to let you leave the bag where it is. However, rules have been created for a reason. That is to keep passengers safe. If you don't like the rules, write the FAA a letter or drive to your destination. Now for full disclosure, a lot of Flight Attendants cite FAA rules that don't exist. I don't know if they intentionally make them up or if it's from ignorance. A company rule is not a federal rule. Just make all of our lives easier and follow the rules.

#65

Buy Seats Together

A lot of airlines sell a very cheap fare class now days. The problem is that those tickets do not get to pick their seats ahead of time. The majority of the time those tickets get the middle seats. That might not be a problem for some travelers, but if you have a family of 4 that can be a problem. The gate agents often do not have seats available to sit you all together. No one wants their toddler sitting with strangers, so most of the time the gate agent says to tell the flight attendant and they will help you sit together. I overheard that one time and told the gate agent I most certainly would not. He would need to fix the issue at the gate. He was annoyed until I explained how we do not have enough time to do that mid boarding. After I explained that, he understood the problem it causes to pass seating issues off on the flight attendants. We will do the best we can especially when small children are involved. Just know, we are on a time crunch to get that door closed on time. Save yourselves the headache and stress and pay a little extra to sit together. Your peace of mind is worth the money.

#66

Hands To Yourself

Passengers don't usually get handsy with a bald, fat 42-year-old, so this isn't an issue I deal with. However, many of my female coworkers do. They have had passengers poke, grab, or grope them. Most of the time, it is just people wanting to get their attention. As people tell every toddler, use your words. You do not need to touch a Flight Attendant to get their attention. If all else fails, push the call light button. They will come and see what you need. If you are touching them to be creepy, just stop. It's disgusting and sometimes people do it to be funny, which is not funny at all. Act like an adult not an animal. As I write this, I do recall a passenger inappropriately touching me. This woman was in first class probably in her late 60s. She motioned for me to bend down to her level. Then she kissed me on the cheek. The first thing the other first-class passengers around her asked was, "is she drunk?" Not like one passenger, but several passengers asked me that. Insulted, I was like," NO!!" Like what the heck. I wasn't offended by the kiss but was by everyone else's reactions. To answer the question, she was not drunk. The next time you need to get a Flight Attendant's attention and want to poke them. Move that finger up to the call light and poke the button.

#67

I'm Not Gay!!

I know that statistically speaking male Flight Attendants are most likely gay. However, we are not all gay!! If you're a gay male Flight Attendant, more power to you. However, for those of us romantically challenged as it is, this is an even bigger obstacle. You can be chatting with a female, and she can seem to be interested in you. Then when she asks that fateful question of, "so what do you do?", it all goes downhill from there. As soon as you say Flight Attend, you know you've lost her. You don't need to finish the word attendant. You can see in her eyes, that she is mentally putting you in the forever friend zone. Not just the let's be friends and see what happens. The he is someone that I can never and will never be attracted to. Some will even say, "omg, my cousin is gay. I should totally set you up." That's when you explain you are not gay. She is embarrassed but you can see you are forever in the eternal prison of the friend zone never to return to possible soulmate island. So ladies, the next time you see a male Flight Attendant, think of the possibility he could be the one for you, not the one for your brother.

#68

Your Life Event Is Not Your Golden Ticket

There is this misconception that if you tell gate agents or Flight Attendants that you are getting married, just got married, got engaged or are celebrating your anniversary you'll get something for free. The internet has led people to believe you'll get upgraded to first class. First of all, let me tell you that First Class is highly overrated at US Airlines. It has a bigger seat and free booze along with slightly better snacks. First class is almost always full now days as it is, with several people on the upgrade list stuck back in poverty class. The odds of you jumping ahead of them are less than 0. They watch the upgrade lists like a hawk and the gate agent would be crucified if you got the seat over them. If there was an open seat you aren't getting it anyways. I think most people wouldn't upgrade someone because they told them something where the obvious intent is to get something free. A gate agent asked me once if he could upgrade this family. I asked why. He said the wife said they should be upgraded because the flight was late. I asked him if the rest of coach was not affected by the delay or just this family was. Needless to say, they did not get upgraded. I'm not giving you free booze either. Buy it yourself or guilt those around you to do it. Or better yet, purchase a seat where alcohol is included. Once there was this Flight Attendant who was notorious for being angry at crewmembers for taking the snacks for sale. One pilot loved M&Ms, and she would never let him have any. If people take things, they are responsible for the consequences of their actions. I am not there to play security guard for M&Ms. We are ready to push back from the gate and she grabs the phone and starts reading something. "Hey baby, we finally are on our way. I can't believe it. I love you so much and I'm happy we are together. Happy Anniversary baby!!" I am standing there with this look of WTF. She then stretches the phone cord to row 2 as they are sitting in row 5. "We will give you some wine. You're 21, right?" This woman who polices pilots taking M&Ms is giving away free booze to some passengers. I am working coach and get to their row during the beverage service. I ask, "how long have they've been married?" "We aren't married. We've been dating for 2 months." I didn't give them anything for free and the other flight attendant got an earful after my

70

service about her stunt. Lesson of the day: don't ask for free stuff. We don't care that your cat is getting married.

#69

Think Before You Stink

This is another one that should be common sense but is not. Don't bring smelly food on the plane. You stink up several rows and then when you throw it away, you make the galley smell. Some food that people bring on the plane smells like death and dirty diaperbalaya, Have some consideration. This doesn't really need much further explanation as it is simple. Bring bland odorless food or eat when you get there. Everyone will be glad you did. A lot of times the smelly food creates a bathroom issue as well. If you skip the stinky food, you are saving your fellow travelers from a possible double olfactory attack.

#70

Take A Shower

I feel like I am a middle school teacher saying this. Please take a shower before you fly. When a flight is an early morning flight, a lot of people either shower the night before or don't shower in the morning. Please stop that foolishness. You smell really bad. Your bath in deodorant or cologne is only making it worse. I understand if you are connecting from an international flight, you are gonna be a little stinky. However, if you started your day in Richmond and it's 5 am you have no excuse. One of the worst offenders was this military analyst from one of the cable news networks. He was rude to begin with but his stench was even worse than his horrible personality. Don't be General Stinky take a shower.

#71

Acknowledge Crewmembers When You Board

Almost every Flight Attendant says hi to every passenger who boards the aircraft. Unfortunately, not all passengers return the greeting. Some will look at you, some will ignore you or some will talk to the person traveling with them. It's very rude. The biggest offenders are women who I call Milwaukee 8s. They are typically women who are reasonably good looking but not supermodel hot. They might be an 8 in Milwaukee but not anywhere else. This is not a dig at the women of Milwaukee but just a city chosen at random. They might have been a cheerleader or a popular girl in their town. Boys probably swooned when they saw her. She was told she was pretty and special, so she developed an attitude. In her mind, all men who initiate or attempt to initiate conversation only do so for purposes of hitting on her. That is despite the fact she is not nearly as attractive as she thinks she is. I want to yell, "I am just saying hello because my employer requires me to. I am not hitting on you so don't flatter yourself." Once one was really rude when she boarded. Flight Attendants are naturally petty people and that day pettiness won out. She went to the first class bathroom before the flight pushed back. After she was done, the Flight Attendant waited

until she had returned to her 6th row seat. They opened the lavatory door and started gagging and acting like they were gonna throw up. They slammed the lavatory door and fake gagged their way back to the galley. They could see she was really embarrassed. Full disclosure, the lavatory did not smell at all. So next time you board, say hi to the Flight Attendant.

#72

The Tale Of Two Cookies

One of the most annoying types of passengers are people who want more than one snack. Not that wanting more than one snack is a problem because it isn't. If you ask nicely, I'll give you as many snacks as I can. It's the people who feel the need to give you this long Lord of the Ringsesque reason why they need 2 snacks. We honestly don't care. This isn't a business loan you are asking for and need to give a long business plan. All you need to do is ask if you can have more than one. We don't need to hear this long tale of woe on how you were going to have lunch but you got caught in traffic so you couldn't stop along the way. Then tell us the ticket counter was so backed up and security took even longer. You were planning to eat at the airport, but you had to rush to the gate just to make the flight. We don't care at all. Please spare us having to hear your most likely made up tale because you didn't want to pay airport prices for food. We don't blame you one bit. Airport food is priced astronomically high. Just ask and ye shall most likely receive.

#73

This Isn't The Price Is Right

Only Bob Barker and now Drew Carey can say come on down. Actually, I think it's the announcer but nobody knows who they are. Don't move yourself to the premium coach seats or first class. I know some of you think you're slick and can just move there and think we won't notice. We have apps that tell us where everyone is supposed to be seated. First class is almost always completely full. If you move to first class, you will be in someone else's seat. When we have to ask for your boarding pass and see you're supposed to be in 18D, you'll look foolish. Someone once tried to play it off that they were confused. I'm like really? 4 and 18 are the same? You sat in A. You didn't even sit in the right letter. The biggest problem are the premium coach seats. A little bit more legroom, free booze and an outlet have turned many a coach passenger into an attempted invader. Most passengers pay extra for those seats, so it isn't right for you to think you can move for free. I had a lady once argue with me and tell me she couldn't believe the airline would allow the seats to go empty. I'm like, there will be an empty seat on the flight either way. Why would they give you something you didn't pay for? She asked if I really was going to make her move. I informed her the plane wasn't moving until she did. She said it was empty. I said so was first class, so why didn't she move there? She said it was because it costs more. I said exactly, like the seat you are sitting in. I said see all these people around you. They all paid extra to sit in these seats. Is it fair to them you moved here for free? They all stared at her, and she begrudgingly moved. The lesson is stay in the seat you paid for because you will be moving back to it if you decide to invade premium seat land.

Learn About Where You Are Going

It seems like a lot of people are traveling and have no idea about where they are going. Once, I was on a train in the UK and a fellow American was attempting to pay for snacks with dollars and then euros. Neither of which are the currency of the UK. I was embarrassed as a traveler and an American. Unfortunately, a lot of those ignorant behaviors are becoming common among people traveling within the United States. I often get asked questions about places we are flying to, like I am somehow their airborne version of Ask Jeeves. Young folks, that was like a prehistoric Google. The most humorous example of that involved a mother and daughter seated next to me on a flight to Grand Forks, North Dakota. I asked why they were headed to Grand Forks. They informed me that they were from Baltimore and the daughter wanted to check into attending the University of North Dakota. I asked if they had ever been there before, and they said no. I asked if they knew anything about Grand Forks. Again, they answered no. I informed them Grand Forks gets cold, like really freezing cold. I said Grand Forks is a city that basically ends and becomes an open prairie. I said the tallest building in town is only around 9 or 10 stories. They laughed and didn't believe me. I said that there are two hobbies that help people survive UND, hockey and alcohol. We started our descent and there was a low layer of clouds obscuring the ground. As soon as we dropped below the clouds, the daughter looked out the window and her mouth dropped. The mom looked at me and said, "you weren't lying. There's nothing here." I said that I had warned them. The daughter started crying and said she didn't want to go there and wanted to go home. As we waited for the hotel shuttle, I saw them waiting as well. The mom informed me that it would have been a several hundred dollar change fee, so they were stuck there for 3 days. They both looked miserable. Don't be them. Do your research.

#75

Don't Ask For The Announcement

If the flight is even the slightest bit delayed, it never fails, someone will ask for me to make an announcement for people with connections to be able to deplane first. I always tell them that I will, but it will not produce the outcome they are hoping for. On regional jets, almost everyone has to leave their roller bags on the jetbridge because they will not fit onboard. You then must claim them at the arrival city on the jetbridge. If you deplane first, you will more than likely still have to wait for your bag anyways. Not to mention, people rarely stay seated. A lot of times, the people most desperate for me to make this announcement will most likely miss their connection no matter when they deplane. The aircraft door at most airlines usually closes 10 minutes prior to departure. The majority of the time, the passenger will tell me they have some impossible time to connect, like 12 minutes and it's 2 concourses away. Usain Bolt, after downing a gallon of Red Bull, couldn't make that happen. I inform them, but they beg me to make it anyways. I do and look up their flight later to see there was no way they made it. There is another thing that goes along with this, that is super annoying. Flight Attendants do not have any way to call your next gate and let them know that you are on your way. You would think with the improvements that have been made in technology, that it would be possible, but it is not. It happens all the time, passengers ask me to call their next gate. They always think that I am lying and ask again. They are almost begging at that point. I inform them that their next gate agent can see where they are on their computer screen. Your seat will change colors if you have a close connection or if you will miss your connection. If the gate agent chooses to wait, it is dependent on a variety of factors along with their supervisor having a say as well. Even if we could call, there would be no guarantee they would wait for you. Please don't ask for the stay seated announcement, for Flight Attendants to call your next gate and don't have unrealistic expectations about making connections.

#76

It Is Possible To Make A Turn Without Stopping

I drive a lot, and this is one of the many road related issues that drive me bonkers. It seems in order to make a turn of any type; some drivers are under the belief they need to make an almost complete stop to do it. I have come close to rear ending several people, because of me not expecting them to make a stop when they could just turn. It's pretty simple, slow down and make the turn. It's not hard at all. The people making u turns are even worse. They make a stop then slowly turn like they're trying to steer the Titanic. I have once been told that I make u turns like James Bond. Apparently, that was not meant as a compliment. There needs to be a happy medium between me and u turns that you could time with a calendar. Drivers are crazy now days. Don't make things harder by being slow and causing accidents.

Green Means Go

If you are first in line for a turn arrow, you have a moral obligation to gun it as soon as it turns green. That way, as many people as possible can make the turn arrow. Instead, we have the first person not paying attention or someone in the middle of the pack clueless and almost no one makes it. The worst is when the last person who makes it, is the person who created the problem. It's their fault. They should have to suffer another cycle of lights like the rest of us. Next time you are in line for the green arrow, get that foot ready on the gas pedal. Don't do it for you, do it for the 11 people behind you who don't have all day to wait for the next few cycles of green lights. It's the right thing to do.

#78

Check In On Crazy Posters

We all have friends who post crazy things on social media. Some are dark, some are just wrong, and some are crazy. Everyone has a different sense of humor. It may seem like you are bothering them but ask them if they are ok. Some people will be mad. Some will say they are ok, and others will be glad you cared and tell you their problems. This is one of those situations where it is better to risk getting them mad, than not reaching out to someone potentially in trouble. I had a coworker who I was friends with. She had a very dark sense of humor. It was dark and sometimes really wrong but funny. I would check in from time to time and she would say she was ok and say that she just had a dark sense of humor. I will never forget when someone messaged me to tell me she was gone. She had been depressed and overdosed on pain medicine. I had tried to check in on her shortly before that, as she had recently been fired from her job. I will never know if I had been able to connect with her, if it would have changed anything. I will always wonder if I or anyone else could have saved her. Don't live with that regret like I do.

#79

Be Real Online

Everyone likes to cultivate their image online. People like to portray themselves as having no problems and everything being awesome. That is a myth and you're a fraud. We all have struggles. Your false reality may cause someone else to compare themselves to you and feel more depressed. Meanwhile, you're struggling yourself. I have a friend who has had struggles, and he is very real. He doesn't sugar coat things, but he doesn't play the victim either. These are his struggles, and he talks about how he is working through them. Some of them are related to mental health which takes bravery to share. As a Christian, it is an even bigger act of bravery as many Christians view mental health issues as a lack of faith or some sort of weakness. He has inspired so many people with his honesty and openness. That sort of thing takes a lot of guts to admit. Be like him and be real. You will never know who you might inspire to keep fighting.

#80

Be Honest Like Abe

Honesty is the best policy the saying goes. The problem with that is while it is the best policy many people do not understand the consequences that come with their honesty. If you are truly honest, you will face backlash a lot of times. People do not always want the truth. They want what will make them feel better or back up their opinion. If you are committed to a reputation of honesty, be ready and be brave. I have a reputation of honesty which has not always been easy. As someone once told me, "People don't always like you or what you have to say, but they know you won't lie to them, and they listen to you." Be the person who people can trust what you say even if they don't like it.

#81

Shop Around

This is easier to do than in the past, but before you make a sizable purchase, shop around. A lot of times you won't save much but occasionally you'll find a great deal. At least by attempting to shop around, you will save yourself the regret of later seeing it for much cheaper. Most of the time people use this philosophy only with big ticket purchases like electronics, appliances and automobiles. One of the biggest parts of a family's budget that has gone up are groceries. Two places that will help you save for groceries are Aldi and Lidl. They are both no frills grocery stores, but you will save a lot. You might have to buy their brand items for much of your order, but you will save considerably over other grocery chains. The way grocery prices have skyrocketed, these two places have helped a lot of people who are struggling to put food on the table. They might not be for you, but those places are worth checking out to see if you could be saving money.

#82

Reusable Bags Are Bad For The Environment

I am sure the people who buy reusable grocery bags mean well. However, their purchase is not as good for the environment as they thought. Reusable bags are responsible for a rise in fossil fuel usage and auto emissions. How, might you ask? You probably always thought that reusable bags were good for the environment. Well, it's because when people use reusable bags at the store, they hold up the line. Most of the time, they are very picky on what goes in each bag. It makes the people behind them wait a long time needlessly. This is where the increase in pollution comes in. The people behind them who have been forced to wait, now have to drive faster to get where they are going. If they are working for one of the grocery delivery services, they really have to go faster to ensure that they are on time. Your purchase to save the planet actually hurts it, so please stop.

#83

Never Enter The Comments

The biggest mistake one can make is entering the comments on any post or article. It never ends well. The kindest, most peace-loving person can become the target of an attack from a stranger who disagrees with them. I don't recall who said it, but someone said the problem is people make comments that they would never make to someone's face. It is true that many people have keyboard courage. They aren't afraid of being held accountable for their actions or being punched in the mouth. I know someone who lost their job because they got into an argument online with a stranger. The person didn't like their comments and sent them to their employer. Both parties should have walked away, but they got heated and couldn't agree to disagree. The next time you feel like commenting just scroll on and watch the chaos unfold. You won't change anyone's mind by commenting anyways.

#84

Be A Clickbait Hero

Click bait articles usually have something to catch your attention. You are intrigued and want to find out the outcome of the featured story, so you click. Often times, the original story isn't even there or takes tons of clicks through ads to get there. Thankfully, there are people who will read the article and save everyone time by posting a screenshot or writing a summary for you. Unfortunately, there will come along an article that tons of people will comment on. They will only post a few words, like great story or I remember when this happened. They often bury the heroes who try and save everyone's time. Don't be those people. Only comment if you're saving people time. Don't tell everyone your opinion on the story, or anything else that is not saving time.

#85

Date Someone For Their Personality

This goes against our beauty culture but date someone not for their looks, but for who they are as a person. This is mostly directed at men, but women can be vain as well. It is also mostly for younger people than older people. A lot of older people have learned this lesson the hard way. I know plenty of great people who are not given the chances they deserve by people they are attracted to because of their looks. I know someone who turned down this great guy who was their friend that was in love with them. Instead, they settled for someone who looked better but treated them horribly. A divorce later, they still haven't learned their lesson. That's why I think someone should create a dating app where there are no pictures. You go through a long process and fall in love with who the person is. At the end of the journey, their looks may still matter but not nearly as much as they do on a picture centric swiping app. It might help reduce the divorce rate in this country and create stronger relationships.

#86

Lower Mileage Is Better

A lot of people get a car because it looks cool. It doesn't matter to them how old the car is. They feel that they need a car that looks cool. Many of them will buy old (not classic) cars with high miles because they look cool. They end up spending a lot of money to fix it. There is no need to overspend on a used car. No one cares that you have a BMW or Mercedes. You aren't impressing anyone with a 15-year-old former luxury car that has 200,000 miles on it or with leather so worn it is smooth. You are wasting money to impress no one. Get the lower mileage car that fits within your budget. No one will be impressed with either car but at least this one will be reliable.

Don't Compare Yourself

It is no longer a popular saying but, in the past, people were said to be trying to keep up with the Joneses. It meant trying to outdo your neighbors or friends. People have always tried to look more successful than the people around them. A lot of people waste time and energy comparing themselves and their situation to other people. They feel inferior or like a failure if they aren't doing as well as other people. It adds unneeded stress on people and their relationships. There are plenty of mansions without furniture in them because someone bought a house to impress people but can't afford to furnish it. There are always people more successful than you, and there are always people worse off than you. You are someone else's definition of success even if you don't feel like it. You don't know the problems of people you view as successful. Don't let their appearance affect your personal outlook. Just relax and do what makes you happy. You don't have to worry what everyone else is doing. You won't feel the need to compete. You can be at peace with your situation.

#88

The Only Color That Matters

In this country, race and color have played a big role. Unfortunately, it has not been a good role. One of the places that it has had a negative impact is the workplace. People are not given chances based on the color of their skin. I am here to tell you there is only one color that should matter. I am sure you are waiting to read something racist. I hate to disappoint you but the color that matters most is green. That does not mean pro Shrek. He would be a terrible employee that would scare customers away. Any smart person in hiring should look at each candidate not at who they are as a person but at their ability to generate green for the company. Thankfully, companies look less at race than in the past. However, there are still stories on how certain names are not given a chance based on their background and perceived potential as an employee. If I ever have a company, your ability to create green for both me and you will be the only color that matters. If you own a company, you should feel the same way.

#89

Don't Change Passwords Early

Changing passwords is the most annoying part of having access to various online accounts. There are so many requirements now. 1 Upper case, 1 lower case, 1 symbol, at least 8 characters, can't be a person or thing, can't be similar to any of your last 115 passwords. There are so many rules and what you have access to isn't anything anyone would really want access to anyways. The thing that annoys me more than changing the password is the frequency in which they want you to change it. In the past, you had to do it every once in a while. Now, one of my accounts wants it changed every 60 days. It sends a reminder to change it like 30 days from expiring every single day until it expires. The sooner I change it, the more often I will have to change it. Why on earth would I want to have to change it more often? That is doubly annoying. Don't give in to the prompts. Stay strong and keep your password until the last day. If you are someone who has the power to enact password policy change, please be merciful and change the rules. It's hard enough to remember passwords without having to remember a new one all the time. Let us keep our passwords longer and reuse old ones!!

#90

Don't Play The Status Card

Airlines give out status to recognize a customer's loyalty. There are many levels based on how much you fly, and in some cases, how much you use their airline branded credit card. Each level comes with certain perks and free upgrades to either a better economy experience or first-class seats. It becomes a problem when the status gives a customer a sense of entitlement. I'll be honest, I won't treat you any differently if you are no status or the highest level. I try and give the best possible service to everyone. You never know the person who isn't an elite member but could bring business to your airline because they were treated well as a "regular" passenger. So, when you tell me something and mention your status it won't matter and in many cases I will become annoyed. Flying 3 times to Rome last year isn't going to change whatever answer you didn't like, to one that will make you happy. We have rules and policies for a reason. It is to ensure everyone is treated consistently. If you ding me to ask if you should upgrade yourself because you are super awesome plutonium class on a 40-minute flight to a better economy seat I am going to be irritated. I do not have the authority to upgrade you. no matter how many times you tell me your status level. The biggest offenders are not the higher levels but the lowest level elite. They will ask for so many things like you are their servant. I have several experiences witnessing status entitlement but two stand out. The first one, I was a passenger and waiting in line at the gate counter. The gentleman in front of me was berating the gate agent because he did not get upgraded to first class. He kept insisting he should be upgraded because he was elite. The agent finally had enough of his behavior and informed him that of the 70 passengers, 60 were elite members and roughly 50 of them were ahead of him on the upgrade list. The second time involved a passenger who was the second lowest tier of elite. He started our conversation by informing me of his status. Then he asked if his travel companion sitting in coach could join him in first class. He again mentioned his status level. He was not happy when I said no. He did not mention it again but did take the time to write a letter complaining about me. I had a meeting with my manager, and I noticed that his letter never mentioned him expecting a free upgrade. Once I informed my manager of what had happened. The meeting was over and I did not get in trouble. The lowest levels will almost always be the ones to mention their status. Which is the opposite of what I thought would happen. The highest levels usually are the most no nonsense just get me there kind of passenger. When I see the flight paperwork, I can usually estimate how the flight will be based on the number and levels of those flying that day. On flights to upstate NY from NYC the low-level elites will often work you to death because on their previous flight they weren't upgraded. They will ask for a predeparture alcoholic drink, ask to see the snack basket twice while in flight and have chug down 2 drinks. Don't be that person. Keep your status to yourself and don't act entitled. You will get the best service I can offer you, no matter who you are.

#91

Be The Hottie In The Pic

If you are going to be on a dating app, don't take group pictures. If you have to include one, don't take one with your most beautiful friends. I know that sounds vain and shallow, but let's be honest. People on dating apps are looking for looks and not character or personality. That's why your profile content is 97% photos. I have seen profile pictures, and you think the profile is for the most attractive person in the pictures. Then you click through the pictures, and it is not. That causes the person who looked at your profile to swipe left. They may have been attracted to you, if it was only you in the other pictures. This is in no means critiquing your looks. I know I certainly not qualified to judge anyone else's looks. I am saying set yourself up for success. Don't give people someone to compare you to. Make your profile about you and the awesome qualities you have to offer. You are your own treasure waiting to be discovered.

#92

Special Orders Do Upset Us

For years, Burger King has had a slogan about having it your way. They have a song and one of the verses says, "Special Orders Don't Upset Us". That is a lie. Fast food is about speed and efficiency. This is made possible by having everything standard. Special orders slow down the process. It is frustrating and takes more time. That in turn, causes you or those dining with you to have to wait longer to get your food. I personally cannot eat raw white onions. I get a headache. Do I special order my Whopper without them? No, I do not. I pick them off and throw them away. It makes it easier on the kitchen staff and helps the process continue to flow smoothly. Some customers will special order their fries without salt, so the kitchen staff has to make new fries for them. Don't do that. It makes more work for the kitchen staff. I am cursed with picking up food for special ordering people all the time. I always have to check to make sure it was made correctly. I know if it is annoying for me as a customer dealing with it one time in a day. It must be really annoying to deal with that several times a day as a restaurant employee. Order your food as it was meant to be consumed. Don't be the one holding up the line.

#93

Don't Have A Teacher's Pet

It seems like every few days in the news, there is a teacher arrested for having an inappropriate relationship with a student. When I was in high school it was almost always a male teacher and a female student. Now, it is almost always a female teacher and a male student. The teachers are usually quite pretty and young. They are women who would have no problem attracting men of the legal age. For whatever reason they go after boys much younger than them. It shouldn't have to be said for either male or female teachers but don't have relationships with your students. That's not even taking the creepiness into account. It's purely for the inappropriateness of your position and the power you have in that position over the other person. That should be common sense but sadly it seems not to be. It isn't worth throwing your life and job away.

#94

Read The Signs!!

If you are in the airport and need to know the location of baggage claim, a gate, another concourse, the restroom, food court or anything you could possibly need. They created these things called signs. Read them!! They are most often overhead. It isn't difficult or an Indiana Jonesesque adventure for the lost city of baggage claim. The signs are everywhere to guide you. Do not approach flight crew who are most likely in a hurry, to ask them questions you could find the answer to yourself. Do not get mad that they are not experts of whatever airport you are currently located in. Most of them only fly in and out and haven't taken a class to be an expert on that airport. Don't make stupid comments about how you cannot believe they don't know. When someone comes up to me and asks a question, I usually have the same response. If they are just lazy, I always seem to be standing under a sign. I reply, "well the giant sign above me says to go this way." They get embarrassed and go on their way. Obviously, if they are elderly, disabled or most likely new to our country, I help them right away. Their request is out of necessity and not laziness. Sometimes if their English is limited it is a challenge, but it is still possible to help them. Once I had a non-English speaking passenger. I called someone I knew who spoke their language. I spent around an hour after my trip helping them get to their next flight on another airline. I even helped interpret for the other airline's gate agent since the passenger missed their flight because we arrived late. Don't bother us with things you should be able to figure out on your own. Unless of course, you're one of the people I have said are ok to ask for help. Then feel free to ask away. If I have time, I may even walk you where you need to go.

#95

Walk Faster

In the airport, about 90% of the people in the concourse are in some sort of hurry. They are trying to catch flights, hurrying to baggage claim, running to the restroom, in a hurry to get food or just in a hurry. The other 10% are the walking equivalent of Sunday drivers. They don't have a care in the world and walk slower than a snail with a broken leg. It's fine that some people walk slow, because we all aren't able or need to go fast. The problem is when the traveling tortoises walk in the middle of the concourse in a serpentine path. It makes it almost impossible to get around them as they move in your way just as you are about to pass them. Since the tortoises are most likely not going to speed up, I have one simple request. Stay on the side of the concourse as you walk. You will not create a traffic jam and will not make it more difficult for those of us who need to be somewhere. If you do this, everyone wins and people can get where they need to go and maybe make their connection.

#96

No Dirty Pictures

If you are looking for a job or a partner don't post naughty pictures on your Facebook page or dating profile. I have friends who are on dating apps tell me that women will state in their profile they aren't about hookups. Then 98% of their pictures are of them in lingerie. No one will do it, but I want someone to ask them if that is their church lingerie. There is nothing wrong with having those pictures if that's what you want to do. You are just sending mixed messages by saying you aren't about sex and post only sexy pictures. If you are looking for a job it most likely won't keep you from getting the job. You will however have creepy coworkers find your page and share your pictures with your other creepy coworkers. There is one consequence that is entirely preventable. It happens to men as well, but it is mostly women. They pose for or take naked pictures and somehow their boyfriend, husband or ex shares them. Then their naked pictures are all over the world. A lot of times, they have no idea that creeps all over the world are looking at them. Don't take naked pictures or videos for anyone. No matter how many times they beg or try to coerce you to do it to prove you love them. Never, ever, ever, ever do it. There is no undo button on the internet. It is out there forever. I know of someone who had posed for pictures and years later if you searched you could find her. Sometimes it happens accidentally, because of a phone or computer being hacked. Other times it is revenge or some other perverted reason. There is no way to 100% ensure what is private stays private. Just don't do it. Just remember, nothing ever dies once it's on the internet. So, if you share, just consider the possible outcomes. I know of a former coworker who posed for pictures once and almost 20 years later they're still making the rounds online. Not everyone can turn a naughty video into a career like a certain family.

#97

Act Like You Belong

I have always believed that if you act like you belong somewhere, no one questions if you do or not. I had a job where I needed to go into the backrooms on weekends of chain department stores. No one ever questioned me, because I walked in there like I belonged. The vendors who came in and acted confused always were questioned. The same thing holds true for better seats at sporting events and concerts. If you act like you are in the right section, then no one will question it. If you are in someone else's seat, you are out of luck if they bring an usher. You can use this at parties and other places that you don't belong. But you better not try it on an airplane though. We watch the premium seats like a hawk. You better believe you will be caught and shamed back into your correct seat. I have been amused by some of the responses from people I have caught. One said that they wouldn't order anything too expensive if I let them stay. I told them no and they told me they thought I was cool. So, try my theory and live it up, but not on the plane because that will never work.

#98

Use Kiosks

Whenever possible use a kiosk. It is almost always faster and more efficient than dealing with a human. I know some people, most of them older, that are on some sort of strike against using them or are afraid of technology. Kiosks are a way better experience. I can zip through the line a lot quicker. This is especially true at movie theaters. It seems like no one will ever use the kiosk. Everyone stands in the long line for tickets, and I zip right past. It even works for tickets you have bought ahead of time online. The next time you have the choice between a person or a kiosk, use the kiosk. It will not cost someone their job like you are told will happen. Most places are so short staffed that they encourage you to use the kiosk. You aren't making some big political statement by refusing to use them. You are wasting your own time. Which is fine with me, because I'll have a shorter line at the kiosk.

#99

Let People Go Ahead Of You

It seems like everytime that I'm at the grocery store. I'll have 4 items and the person in front of me at the checkout has 172. Some of the time and it seems like less and less often, they will let me go ahead of them. That is the courteous thing to do. Unfortunately, the majority of people will look at you once or twice and see that you have considerably fewer items than them. Instead of offering to let you go ahead of them, they will develop some sort of neck condition that will make it impossible to look back in your direction. It is super comical. It looks really uncomfortable for them. They will do anything to avoid making eye contact because they know they are in the wrong. If they do accidentally make eye contact, I'll give them a big smile. That usually makes them feel guilty and they try even harder not to look at me. It's not the end of the world for me to have to wait. It's just the polite thing to offer. Be the good person and let the person with less items go ahead. Don't be the inconsiderate person.

#100

Don't Abandon Your Friends

Friends and more specifically good friends are harder to come by now days. It seems loyalty only exists as long as times are good. My sister was in a bad accident in high school. She had a long recovery and you found out who her true friends were. People visited at first but slowly less and less visited. The road to recovery was long and the number of friends who were there at the end was significantly less than at the beginning. Be a good friend. Don't abandon your friends when times get tough. I know someone who seems to cycle through friends often. They will be friends with them and it's all about that friend. Then something happens and you never hear about them ever again. If you ask about that friend, there is always some convoluted and farfetched story where the other person is always at fault. Don't be that friend. Be a friend in good times and in bad. You can help them get through the problem and they can be there when you need someone to lean on. Sometimes the friendship can be one sided, but at the end of the day you are being a good friend whether or not that loyalty is reciprocated.

#101

Corn Nuts Yuck!!

If you ever eat Corn Nuts in public, you are one of the worst humans who have ever lived. They smell absolutely horrible. They are one of the worst smells I have ever smelled. It is even worse when people eat them on the airplane. Half the plane reeks of this wretched smell. It makes me wanna puke everytime. The next time you have the urge to buy Corn Nuts to eat in public, don't!! Eat them at home and eat them alone, very far away from any other human. Don't be a terrible person and certainly don't ever think of eating them on a plane.

#102

Hold Your Important Stuff Close

A lot of travelers are unfamiliar with regional jets and do not realize that they may have to gate check their luggage. Once they realize that, they are often rushed to take valuable things out of their bag. They often forget keys, phones, medicines and computers. Checked baggage is often not treated with the love and respect it is by its owner onboard the plane. It is also stacked beneath or on top of other bags making anything breakable at risk of being damaged. Most aircraft have closets that Flight Attendants can use to store fragile items. Once, there was a woman who was upset about having to gate check her luggage. She was pleading with the gate agent to be able to bring it on the flight. The gate agent refused. During the flight, I found out that the woman's mother had passed away. The items in the bag were her mother's possessions. They were pictures and other sentimental items. I apologized, because if I had known that was the case. I would have insisted we find room for her belongings. Another time, I had a flight that was the last flight of the day from Cincinnati. When we arrived at our destination, we learned that all the gate checked bags were left back in Cincinnati. It was 7pm, which meant the next chance for them to retrieve their bag would most likely be 10 am the next day. You may never experience a lost bag, but if you do, you will be glad that you listened to me and were prepared. The airline industry has made great strides over the years in not losing luggage. Unfortunately, it still does occur. Thankfully, it is rare to happen now. I have heard of passengers not having their passport for their next flight. Passengers not having their car keys to drive home. Passengers who are missing medicine that they need but don't have because their bag was lost. I encourage everyone to carry 2 bags. One rollerbag and one bag with your breakables like computers and things like keys, ids, medicines and other items that are important that you can't live without. While airlines try their best to avoid inconveniences the best thing to do is pack, so that the impact of an inconvenience to you is minimal.

#103

I'm Allergic

We are promised in the Constitution to have life, liberty and the pursuit of happiness. Nowhere in the Constitution does it say that your problems should become everyone else's problems. It seems that there are certain allergies where the person who has them is very demanding. They will confront the gate agent and Flight Attendant and demand they police the other passengers and stop them from consuming whatever they are allergic to. The best that we can do is to ask people to be considerate of your allergy. We cannot and will not police everyone. The nut allergy people seem to be the most militant on this issue. A lot of them are downright rude. We have procedures that we follow but telling us that we are required to stop anyone from consuming your allergen is not going to happen. I once had a lady approach the gate agent loudly demanding that we make sure that no one consumes any products with gluten in them. She claimed to have an airborne gluten allergy. None of us had heard of this allergy, so we had to Google it. Apparently, it is extremely rare but if she wore a mask, she would be ok. I will never forget telling the country boy captain and his response. "What in the hell is that?" We ended up taking a delay while higher ups sorted out what to do. She flew with a mask but was very angry at everyone because according to her we should have known. I am unlikely to keep my job after sharing my thoughts with customers, but I will be thinking maybe you shouldn't fly if you use the words highly allergic. Unless you are allergic to Corn Nuts. I will totally enforce compliance with not eating them onboard.

#104

Research The Airline You're Flying On

Generally speaking, most major airlines are close to the same in terms of being on time or canceling flights. They try and tell you that they're different, but they are really not. Truth be told, the only flight that matters if it is on time is the one you are on. If the airline is on time 99% of the time and your flight is the 1%, their statistics are meaningless to you. Where they differ are in their connection carriers. They are called regional airlines but when a "regional" flight goes from one part of the US to a foreign country 3 hours away, the word regional isn't really accurate. If you have a flight on one of these airlines it could make or break your trip. Some regionals have horrendous on time performance and cancelation rates. I don't want to get sued but there are a handful of regional airlines that I would never let anyone I know fly on. I just suggest you Google the regional airline you'd be flying on, before you book. You might save your trip by doing that and avoiding one of them.

#105

I Fly More Than You Do

Probably one of the most annoying things passengers say is, "I fly more than you do". It is beyond annoying. I can promise you that you don't. Somedays I fly 6 flights in a day. A lot of months I fly 60 flights in a month. I can guarantee the number of passengers who fly 700 flights in a year is almost zero. For those who do, thank you for your business. For those who make that comment, thank you for your business. I am glad you fly a lot, but your comment is not unique, welcomed or even remotely close to true. Stop trying to be witty. I'll give you the obligatory chuckle and offer to let you do the beverage service. But know that if I could, I would be rolling my eyes.

#106

Traditions Are Made To Be Broken

Our older relatives seem to believe in the importance of tradition. While traditions can be good, some of them are unnecessary and unwanted. Most of the controversial ones involve weddings and babies. The elders push hard on continuing a tradition that needs to end. It usually involves making the person who is forced to follow the tradition upset, about a life event they should be happy about. It might involve someone being in the wedding that the bride doesn't want. I know of tradition going wrong in my own life. My grandmother and great grandmother were not on speaking terms for almost the entirety of my life. I don't know all of the details, but it had something to do with some baptismal outfit. I believe it was supposed to go to me, but my great grandmother passed it on to someone else. The ironic thing is that my parents are not Catholic and would never have used it as I was not baptized. In the 31 years I was alive during my great grandmother's life, I met her twice. She lived less than 20 minutes away from me the majority of the time. The first time was when I was around 7. My mom and dad wanted my sister and I to meet her and my great grandfather. My great grandmother was worried my grandmother would find out and take it out on us her grandchildren. It saddens me that the tradition robbed me of almost a lifetime of knowing my great grandparents. It saddens me even more that I had to Google to find their names. Don't let traditions take from you what it took from me.

#107

Don't Take Pictures Of People's Guts

In life, there are moments for photos and there are moments where maybe you should check the whole scene before taking the picture. One example would be the miracle of childbirth. If your partner is having a c section, it might be best to not take a picture of the baby coming out with all of mom's insides on display. This may come as a shock to you as it did me, but the mother of the child does not always appreciate that. They really don't appreciate it when you post said picture to Facebook for the world to see. Personally, I think one's internal organs deserve their time to shine but as they are not your organs, you don't get to decide that. Well at least I didn't. I am sure there are many other similar situations where checking the area is best advised before taking and posting a picture. Please use this valuable piece of wisdom whenever you take a picture and avoid the ire of someone in the picture.

#108

Don't Tell Someone They're Bad For Your Image

I think males of all ages believe they have some degree of coolness about them. When you're older, you realize that you've never been cool. I also have been completely clueless when women like me. This story takes place in I believe my sophomore year of high school. I think I'm supposed to change the names, so I don't get sued. I was friends with a girl we will call Mandy for legal reasons. I ate lunch at the same table with her 2 friends. She asked me to the Sadie Hawkins dance. My conservative Christian parents were opposed to dances, so I had to say no. I figured she wanted to go as friends. I certainly did not think she liked me. I had a crush on this tomboy girl in my gym class we will call Tami. She was cute and I think played volleyball. Well, one day in gym class, Tami asked me if Mandy was my girlfriend since we ate at the same lunch table. I had never thought anyone would think that, and yet here my big crush was thinking not that she liked me but that I had a girlfriend. I quickly answered, "NO!!" Occasionally, guys hear phrases they think sound cool. The thing is that they do sound cool, but only in movies when being said by movie stars not when normal uncool guys are repeating it. I had the bright idea to use one. Spoiler alert: it did not end well. I decided to tell Mandy that I could no longer sit by her at lunch as it was bad for my image. Yes, the guy who in his senior pictures looks like he was the athletic trainer for the Chicago Bulls thought he had an image. For some reason, I was shocked, both that she ran to the bathroom crying and that in our next hour biology class a few girls said words Jesus wouldn't like to me as they passed my table. That stupid line haunted me for years, to the point that I thought that she had put some sort of curse on me. I felt bad thinking of how hurtful and moronic I had been. She was a really nice girl, and I was a total jerk. I wasn't even cool enough to get away with being that kind of jerk. If I hadn't been so clueless, I might have seen she liked me, and things could have ended up differently. Years later I found her on Facebook and apologized. She forgave me but I still feel bad. She is married to a great guy, so it all ended well. Life lesson: don't be a jerk and don't overstate your coolness.

#109

Don't Fake An Injury

Another tale of love gone wrong. It is surprising that I have 2 stories regarding dating since I have not been the prolific dater many men have been in their lives. This story takes place in 6th grade. I attended a small Christian school for 5th and 6th grade. In 5th grade, I developed a crush on a blonde girl we will call Cami. In 6th grade, I decided to ask her out. Well since I was and still am terrified of rejection. I had an intermediary ask her out for me. She turned me down. She used words that I have hated since then which may have helped shape my personality. "He's a nice guy but...", I was, as might be expected, devastated. I have always been a planner, so I created a plan to win her love. I had a sling and arm brace from when a few months prior, I got kicked by a kid in recess and sprained my wrist. He was about to throw a football and I stripped it from him. He turned around and kicked me in the hand. He lied and said I pushed him. I most certainly did not. He was a pastor's kid, who typically are troublesome, so his lie checks out. Back to the plot to win love. I had an accomplice who I had told to call Cami during Christmas break. He was to tell her that I got hit by a car while saving a dog. In my 6th grade mind, that was a genius way to win her love. On New Years Day, the accomplice called my house and asked to speak with me. He asked if the plan was a go. I said yes. My parents asked, "why did he call you?" I said, "oh, he was calling to wish me a Happy New Year." I don't know why I thought my parents would believe that 6th graders would call and wish each other Happy New Year, but they did. What is even funnier is that kid had never called me before or after that call. I get to school after Christmas break very excited. I put my sling on, and my accomplice tells me that I have it on the wrong arm. I'm like, why did you tell her a specific arm and why the arm that I write with? I go sit in my desk and she doesn't show up when class starts. I take my sling off since my perfect plan failed because she didn't come to school. Well, I took my sling off too soon, because she was just late for school. She comes into class and sees that I do not have a sling on and figured out it was all a lie. Needless to say, Cami did not fall in love with me or change her mind about being my girlfriend. In fact, she was as angry as a 6th grade girl could get. I think it was pretty romantic for a 6th grader to come up with that plan to win her love. Some may say desperate, but I think if Hallmark had made movies back then, they would have made one out of that.

#110

Take The Risk

One of my biggest regrets in life has been my reluctance to take risks. Whether that be careerwise or in love. I have always made the safe choice. Women that I was too scared to ask out because I didn't want to be shot down. The business ideas I never pursued because I was afraid to fail. As I have gotten older, I have become more willing to take risks. Writing this book is one. Will anyone read it? Will people make fun of it? Will I sell any copies at all? We will see if this becomes a risk that was worth taking or not. At least I will know that I gave it my best shot. Take risks when you are young. You will never know what you will achieve. If you wait until you are older, you don't know what you will miss out on. You will also be more desperate for your older risks to be successful. Accept that failure is a possibility, but it does not have to be a probability, nor does it have to be fatal. Don't let your failures kill your drive to take chances. Do not be afraid to fail but do not get to the point where you expect it. Failure can teach us many things, but do not allow it to demoralize you and stop you. It is a speed bump not a roadblock. Be as educated as you can about risks but do take them.

#111

Don't Give Away The Last Dessert

This isn't really that big of a life lesson. It's more of a complaint. What can I say? Flight Attendants can be petty. You have one dessert left in the freezer. Let's say it was a Reese's Peanut Butter Ice Cream cone. You bought them when they were on sale. No one else in the house liked them so you ate one every few days. You are all excited to come home and have the last one. You open the freezer and to your surprise it is gone. You inquire with your housemates and one of them informs you that they gave it away to a visiting child. The reason being that no one liked them anyways. If there was only one left, that should have been an indication that someone liked them. To give it away is bad enough, but to a child is even worse. You could have given them fruit snacks. I'm still mad and it was like two months ago. I guess the life lesson is that you don't give away desserts to anyone who visits.

#112

Don't Whistle At Women

This is more for the readers from the New York/New Jersey area. Don't cat call women. I didn't know this was actually still a thing until female friends of mine informed me that it was. It is offensive and stupid. Leave women alone. There is no need to be saying things to them. They have enough to worry about concerning their safety than a bunch of neanderthal men shouting things at them. Say nothing or wish them a nice day. Evolve.

#113

Don't Be Rude To People Helping You

One thing that has puzzled me in life are people who are rude to customer service people who are helping them. I want to ask them if they think that by being mean, it will inspire the customer service person to go the extra mile or do the bare minimum. It seems to be very common in the airline industry. Often times gate agents and flight attendants are the personification of the airline. So, we take the brunt of people's anger. Gate agents especially must be saints, because of a lot of things they have said to them. I think most people would rebook the rude people into a middle seat by the bathroom. I was injured once and waiting in an emergency room waiting room. The person at the check in desk next to me was super rude to the hospital person helping them. I was in pain and had enough of their rudeness. I went off on them about how the hospital people were trying to help them, and that they should be nice to them. The next part I probably should have skipped, but I'll blame the pain. I said that someone should wheel them right into Lake Superior. The person shut up and everyone in the waiting room was shocked. I was still in pain but at least that lady wasn't being yelled at anymore. The lesson is to be kind to those helping you. Not because you might get something extra. Not because a stranger might go off on you. But because the people helping you deserve to be treated with respect and kindness.

#114

Pay For The Upgrade

This happens in life in many areas but predominantly it is in air travel. You are given the option to pay for an upgrade. It may be offered to you at booking or check in. Pay for it. So many passengers are unhappy with whatever seat they are assigned. It is too far back, too close to the engines, too close to the bathroom, not enough legroom, the reasons are endless. They end up having regret for passing up the opportunity for a better seat. Some watch the seating options change online like a hawk, in the hopes a better free option becomes available. Almost every time, the better free option never comes. That may be because other passengers have the same idea and snag a better seat before you or because of how full flights are booked. You might have the idea to ask a Flight Attendant as you board for a better seat or try and sneak into an empty premium coach seat. If the flight is almost full in coach, the odds of them being able to move you are almost zero. If you sneak into premium coach, you will be caught and have the embarrassment of being sent back to your original seat. Flight Attendants are not allowed to give you a free upgrade, so don't make it as though they are being unreasonable if they won't move you to an empty seat. On one flight, I noticed a woman had moved herself into a premium coach seat. I said, "you're not in your correct seat, are you?" She responded that she moved seats, because it was open. I informed her that she cannot move herself into a premium coach seat without paying. She said, "you mean to tell me the airline expects the seat to be open". I said that there will be open seats no matter what and the airline doesn't expect the more expensive seats to be given away for free. She repeated her objections again. I said, "there are open seats in first class, why didn't you move there?" "Well, those seats cost extra." I replied, "exactly, just like these seats, so you need to move." "You mean to tell me that you are expecting me to move back to my other seat?", she asked. "I don't expect you to move. I insist that you move". She sat there and wouldn't move. So, I said, "it's not fair to all these people around you who paid to sit up here." The people around her all started to stare at her. She got embarrassed and grumbled while moving back to her correct seat. You get what you pay for. Don't be that lady. Get the better seat but get it by paying for it.

#115

Some People Just Want To Sit Alone

This is a huge pet peeve of Pilots and Flight Attendants. They will find an area of seats where no one is around them in a gate area. It might be a gate where a flight doesn't leave for several hours, or just a less populated gate. They will sit down and get comfortable. It never fails, someone will find the same quiet area and sit down. But not just sit down. They will sit right next to them or behind them. They will almost always be talking on their phone loudly as well. I can guarantee that if you ask most Pilots or Flight Attendants, they will tell you that this is one of their biggest pet peeves. They can probably reference at least several hundred times this has happened to them. It is something we have never been able to figure out. Why on earth with all the seats available, do people sit right next to the one person in this vast sea of nothingness? It is rude and just plain annoying. Let the person seeking quiet, get the quiet they seek. Most importantly, give them the space they seek as well. We are in close quarters with passengers for several hours of our day. We don't have a break room. Give us this oasis of solitude and space. Feel free to take any of the other seats in the area a reasonable distance away. We might not say anything, but we will be silently thanking you.

#116

Don't Be Shady

I don't have a funny story to go along with this one. It really shouldn't need saying but don't be shady. Don't be someone people cannot trust. Everyone knows someone they are related to, friends with or work with that people don't trust. It may be because of something they said or did, but you can't trust them. You can't believe their stories or their reasons for needing help. What's saddest of all, is that usually they have no idea that everyone knows how untrustworthy they are. They think everyone is buying their story, when in reality the people listening are completely writing it off as false. If anyone ever calls them out about it. They get very defensive and some manipulators turn the situation into one where they're the victim. Don't be that person. Be someone people can trust and believe what they say.

#117

Don't Trust A Man Bun

I have no scientific reasoning for this rule but nevertheless, don't trust someone with a man bun. Maybe it is jealousy for my inability to have enough hair for a man bun or I just don't like how it looks. No matter what my deep seeded psychological reason is for my stance. I do not trust a person with a man bun. I'm sorry. Get a haircut or leave your hair down. Once the manbunners read this, I will never be allowed into a fair-trade coffee shop or vegan restaurant ever again. I am heartbroken that I will never have a first visit to either of those types of establishments. That is a sacrifice I must make, to spread my anti man bun views and save humanity.

#118

Green Can Be Bad

Green is a good color for money. When it creeps into your emotions it becomes a bad thing. People become green with envy over every little thing. It can blind people from reality. While sometimes someone's success or good fortune can seem undeserved. You don't see everything that they could be going through. In some cases though, they could still be a terrible person. I had a friend who was not the nicest person. They experienced huge success in their field at a very early age. They were actually a terrible person. They had an affair with someone who was engaged. They treated their parents terribly. They also resented most of their customers and spoke terribly of them. It seemed like the worse their ego got, the more successful they became. I can admit I became very jealous. It was not because of someone having great success, but because I felt it was so undeserved for how they acted as a human. It took some serious introspection to realize that I should be happy for their success and not try to justify my jealousy. I encourage you to be happy not jealous. It may be hard to do at first, but it is possible. Trust me, it was not easy.

#119

Try To Understand Different Vews

There is an old saying, which because of the internet, probably has had its origins debunked. It is allegedly a Native American saying. It speaks of not really being able to know someone, until you walk a mile in their moccasins. I interpret that as not judging someone until you see their view of an issue. There are so many issues that people feel strongly about. There are a lot of people who are opposed to abortion. If you were raped or had a baby that you were told would not survive you might feel differently. It's ok to still be against it, but you can be respectful of those who support it. In 2020, it became two distinct sides. Either you hated the police or supported them unconditionally. There are many people who have police officers in their family who are good officers that are upset about the generalization of all police as bad. Then there are people who are pulled over or harassed because of their race. In some situations, it has even resulted in some innocent people being killed. If both sides could look at the other and see that we do need police reform while also needing to support the police, it would help all of our communities. There are so many different issues this could be apply to. You don't have to agree with someone's beliefs. You should just try to understand them and not see them as the enemy for not having the same beliefs as you.

#120

Don't Eat On Tray Tables

There is a common misconception that airplanes are clean places. During the pandemic, airplane cleaners came through the plane with this glorified mobile smoke machine to "clean" it. However, those days are over. It is back to the days of the dirty plane that's basically just cleaned of visible trash between flights. Sometimes on a flight, someone is changing a diaper on their tray table. The next flight, someone is eating off of the same tray table. People do their nails on tray tables. They do crafts and have all manner of unclean things on the tray tables before you board and put your lunch on it. I have seen people eat straight off the tray table without any napkins in between. That makes me want to puke after seeing what has been on there on the flight before. If you must eat, lay several napkins, food wrappers or bags between your food and the tray table. That might not be part of your brownie on the tray table. Just something to think about.

#121

Vaguebooking Is The Worst

Facebook can be a good thing and a terrible thing. One of the most annoying types of people are vaguebookers. They post about some drama and leave details out. Someone has to ask them what it's all about. They may respond with it's nothing or if by messenger they may give the details. They also might post passive aggressive things that the person they are referring to, either doesn't see or doesn't know it's about them. It always makes me laugh when the person everyone else knows it is about makes a comment supporting it. Like do you not know they are talking about you? One of the biggest offenders of vaguebooking is always posting about boundaries and emotional stuff. Everyone who knows the situation, knows she is talking about a particular family member. The family member is from all accounts, quite a terrible person. However, she has no clue those posts are referring to her. I almost want to comment and say this is about you. She would probably get mad at the poster and make her life worse. It can be so annoying. I just want to tell her to get it out in the open, so we can stop reading this and she can get some resolution. There's the lesson of the day. Call people out directly for their shenanigans. Don't vaguebook.

#122

Don't Use Slang With Non English Speakers

This one really annoys me. I will be out with people, and they will try and make conversation with people which is nice. However, they will often encounter someone where English is not their first language. I feel so bad for the other person in this moment. My friends or family members will use slang or phrases, which you can tell the other person has no clue what is trying to be communicated to them. The person will be completely confused as to what is going on. I will become annoyed because I feel bad for the other person being put in that situation. It is hard to learn a second language and I commend anyone who does that. Unfortunately, in learning a language you often do not pickup slang. The United States has slang by region and even a native English speaker like me can be clueless as to what someone else is trying to say. The same thing can happen on the airplane. A Flight Attendant can be talking to someone from another country, and they have no clue what is going on. I think overall we should try and eliminate slang. I understand that is not likely to happen. We should at least try to be conscious of who we are speaking to and how we might be making communicating difficult for the other person.

#123

The Customer Isn't Always Right

Baby boomers are the ones who ruined customer service. The saying they have chanted like monks, is the customer is always right. They have used that for years with the expectation of getting free stuff. This has caused many customer service employees to become jaded and not give their best service. There is a grocery chain where they go overboard for customers. I worked in the deli and this assistant store manager came over to the deli one day. He said we needed to slice turkey lunchmeat so he could drive it to a customer. She had wanted turkey but got ham. I witnessed what had happened, and she had said ham. She got what she ordered. However, she called and complained to the store. She not only got free lunchmeat but got it delivered for free. The customer service person hadn't made a mistake at all. The woman just abused the system because of her own screw up. This type of behavior may be why your gate agents and Flight Attendants are less than helpful or friendly. I have had customers complain to me expecting me to give them whatever they wanted because they complained. I am sorry about whatever issue they experienced, but I cannot upgrade them to first class no matter how many times they tell me the airline needs to do something. If you have a real issue complain. If you are trying to get something for free from a minor inconvenience don't. You are helping ruin customer service.

#124

Don't Be Gate Lice

There is a term among airline employees for people who crowd the boarding area when it is not their time to board. Those people are called gate lice. A lot of times the previous flight hasn't even deplaned yet, and these people are all lined up ready to board. It is super frustrating, especially if you are trying to get to the counter so you can work the flight. Just sit down and relax until your zone is called. You have an assigned seat. No need to rush or get in the way. It seems like almost everytime that I am trying to board as a passenger, I have to ask 10 people if they are in line so that I am not cutting ahead of them. About 80% of the time, they aren't boarding. They are just in the way. At one airport, the elite members stand against the wall by the elite boarding lane. They line up so early before boarding, that they have to lean against the wall. They will almost always have one leg bent pushing against the wall to hold themselves up. They look ridiculous. I will come off of a flight and the next flight won't leave for an hour. Yet, these people will all be lined up leaning against the wall. Stop getting in the way. Wait in your seat until your zone is called. It will make things easier for everyone. Plus, you won't look ridiculous.

#125

$15 For An Old Sandwich

Airport food is expensive, like really expensive. It usually isn't very good either. There are a few exceptions to this rule. Pittsburgh and one other one airport that I have forgotten, have laws that require businesses in the airport to charge prices found in their locations outside the airport. It is great, because everything is a lot more affordable. They even have a Rite Aid in Pittsburgh, which is great for cheap snacks. In La Guardia, it is around $15 for a premade sandwich, which isn't very good and was made like 3 days ago. That is common in most airports. You may also pay around $15 for a Big Mac meal at an airport McDonalds. The food is never worth the price in terms of quality or service. I suggest you bring food. It may be a sub you picked up on the way to the airport or just snack foods. You won't go hungry, and you will save a lot of money. Who needs to pay $5.79 for a small bag of Cheezits? Columbus, Ohio used to have a Wendy's outside security. They had a dollar menu in the days of dollar menus. I would hurry between flights to get the rare cheap meal. One day, the security line was long, so I got back to the plane at 9 minutes before departure. We were booked full, so it looked like I was headed towards a biggie sized meeting with my manager. Somehow, we boarded all 50 people in 7 minutes and closed the door 2 minutes early. That almost delay would have been avoided if I had brought food. You might not delay a flight getting food in the airport, but you will save time and money if you decide to bring your own.

#126

We Are Not A Destination Information Guide

For some reason, airline passengers think we are experts on every city and airport. Might I suggest our good friend Google. Google can find you all the answers you need. From where baggage claim is, to where to eat in your destination. If we are not based at that airport, we might know where a Starbucks is in the terminal and maybe somewhere good or cheap to eat. Other than that, we know very little about each terminal and city. We go to so many airports and often don't even get off the plane when we are there. Please don't ask us airport specific questions or get mad when we don't know. A lot of cities we try to avoid going to. It might be a year or two since we were last there. Some places we try to forget. On one layover in Bangor, Maine, my crew and I went to see the Duck of Justice. We had Googled what to do in Bangor. Our Uber driver and half of the people we had encountered had never heard of it. He had called his son because he didn't believe the Duck of Justice was real. He even parked his car and came in to see it with us. It was amusing that Google knew more than most of the townsfolk. It is easy for you, to not only find information but also find accurate information. That way you aren't relying on someone who may be confusing Charleston, West Virginia with Charleston, South Carolina.

#127

It's Not Raining In New York

This one annoys both Flight Attendants and Pilots. We will be delayed somewhere for weather. A passenger or three will feel the need to tell us that they called Gertrude in Long Island, and it isn't raining there. They will be angry and will yell at us accusing us of lying, while asking why we aren't leaving. First of all, we aren't getting paid as we sit there with the door open. If I am sitting anywhere with the door open and not getting paid, I want to go just as much as you do. Second and most important of all, we fly when Air Traffic Control says we can go. In places that are busy like New York, they limit how many planes can fly into the airport during bad weather. They make the flights that haven't taken off yet wait, so we aren't forced into a holding pattern on the way and burn gas. That keeps us from diverting for more gas and possibly canceling in another city. We have to wait to leave and once they say we can go we leave. So, while it isn't raining now, those flights who had to wait to land are ahead of us. Next time, just let the ones whose job it is to get you there, follow the proper protocols. Trust that we want to go and also want to start getting paid.

#128

Make Backup Plans

You travel plans can change in an instant. As an airline employee, I travel at space available. That means a seat needs to be empty for me to get one. I commuted to New York for 5 years. I would often fly up on Monday morning to start a trip. I usually would fly home on Friday or Saturday. I would start making my plans and backup plans to go home at the beginning of the week. I would study the forecast and how that would impact both the flights home and the flights I was scheduled to work. I would look at passenger loads and see if I would be able to even get a seat. Then I would look and see what my backup options were. I would see what was available for flying on other airlines or flying through other cities. I would look each day and analyze the updated data. I would constantly change my plans and backup plans. While passengers don't have to worry about getting a seat, they do have to worry about the weather. If you are making a connection, will the weather affect you making your connection? As the weather is considered an act of God, the airline won't be getting you a hotel. Do you change to an earlier flight? Do you book a hotel in your connection city just in case? These are things you need to plan for in your travels. Do you need to be somewhere at a certain time for an event or a meeting? I once had a flight where we deplaned and swapped crews which caused a significant delay. I had a passenger cuss me out because she was heading to a wedding and was going to miss it. If she had planned ahead, or made backup plans, she might have had other options. Instead, she was going to miss out on the entire purpose of her trip. Don't miss out or get stranded because you didn't plan.

#129

Go To Bed Angry

One piece of advice given to newlyweds is that you shouldn't go to bed angry. It sounds nice but in reality, it wastes time and often doesn't really change anything. Often times, one person caves so there can be a peaceful resolution. If someone won't cave, you spend a long time talking and arguing while missing out on sleep. I go to bed angry all the time. I refuse to waste time trying to change my spouse's mind when I am tired. It isn't healthy or good for anyone. If you go to sleep, you can wake up with a new outlook at the issue being argued. Both of you might see things differently. Either way, you are waking up rested and not tired for staying up late just to "agree". You can have a real solution and not one where the other caves just so you can go to sleep. So be mad when you go to sleep. Tell your partner you will pause the argument and revisit the issue in the morning. You can agree to disagree for the sake of sleep. There is plenty of time to fight in the morning.

#130

They Let Me On The Last Plane

The majority of the time this involves situations where passengers want to store their baggage. It is almost always passengers in the front row who want to store their bag in front of their feet. I will inform them that unfortunately that is not allowed by the FAA. They will a lot of times say, "they let me on the last plane". Like if they broke the rules on the last flight, I should allow them to do the same on this flight. However, that's not how it works. First of all, we usually believe you are making your claim up. Some Flight Attendants do not follow the rules, but the majority do. Second of all, we are held accountable for what we do. We cannot use the excuse that a passenger said they were allowed to break the rules on the previous flight. I do not know a single Flight Attendant who would risk getting in trouble just because a passenger gave them an excuse. It is not fair to expect someone to risk discipline, because you do not want to follow the rules. Just follow the rules. There's no need to fight or lie. In the end, you will have to follow the rules. Let's make it easier for everyone.

#131

This Isn't 7-11

There are not a lot of passengers who are like this but some of them have this idea that the galley is a convenience store. They ask for random things. One passenger in first class asked if we had bowls of rice. Another asked if we had extra first-class meals or "some pasta or something". We do not have extra first-class meals and we certainly do not have random foods that we did not serve like pasta or rice. I have had passengers ask for espressos and cappuccinos and are very surprised when I tell them that we do not have them. I have been asked for random drinks and snacks that we do not have. We have canned soda, canned juices, coffee, water and alcohol. We have a limited number and limited types of snacks. We do not have playing cards. We do not have magazines or newspapers. Whatever item that you'll need, you will need to either pickup in the airport ahead of time or wait until we arrive. Please don't ask us for items we don't offer you. The odds are almost 100% that we won't have what you need.

#132

We Don't Know Your Old Neighbor Bob

For some reason, people think everyone in the airline industry knows each other. I work at a small airline where in my department we have around 1600 people, and I don't know the majority of them. The odds of us knowing anyone that you know are slim. It never fails, some passenger will ask if I know their old neighbor Bob. Most of the time they have no clue what airline Bob worked for. A lot of times they'll say they think he's retired now. They don't know what aircraft he flew. They will say he liked to go to Paris. They don't even know where he was based. If you say you don't know Bob, they will feel compelled to give you more information about him. "His wife Carol had cancer some years back and his girls moved back to be close to them." It's great to hear Bob raised such great girls, but I honestly don't know him. I also do not care to continue this conversation. However, my job requires I stand there and hear this insanity. I have always wanted to say, "didn't you hear? Carol left Bob". Then say something scandalous happened or say Bob is in prison. But my luck, they'd write a letter or they know someone important, and I would get in trouble. Please don't ask us if we know Bob. We don't.

#133

Be Honest In All Situations

I believe in being honest in all situations. Sometimes that means being inconvenienced in order to be honest. It might be that I was given extra change or not charged for some small item. I believe that if you cannot be honest in small things. You cannot be trusted to be honest in large ones. Your mind tells you that it is just something small so it doesn't matter, but you will know that you weren't honest. I have stood in long lines several times to be honest. The cashiers are always shocked. It is sad that being honest is now shocking to people. It shouldn't be that way. You cannot act dishonestly and expect others to be honest to you. Be honest in all situations both big and small. It might be inconvenient, but it is worth it.

#134

Don't Take The Last Flight Out

It might be because of cost or convenience but many people take the last flight out of a destination and have a connecting flight. Don't do it. If something goes wrong and you miss your connection, then you are stuck. It might be that the flight is coming in late due to running behind schedule or it might be due to weather. It is a risk you shouldn't take. In Michigan, it is often cheaper to drive to Flint and fly from there. The tickets are sometimes cheaper, and the parking is a lot cheaper. I have experienced the downside of passengers attempting to save money. It would be the middle of winter and we would be delayed. Then we would have to deice delaying us further. The passengers would miss their connection in Detroit. Because it was weather related, the airline did not give them a hotel room. They would be close to home, but without their car. They would also miss a day of being in their destination. Whatever money they saved was not worth the misery they experienced. They would often direct their anger at me. The reality is, they created their own problem. If it had happened earlier in the day, they could have been rebooked if they missed their connection. Instead, they missed the last chance of the night to connect. It's not worth it, don't do it.

#135

Fly Out Of Big Cities

Often times, people are forced to fly to smaller towns. It may be because it is more convenient, but it is almost never because it is cheaper. There is usually very little competition, so the fares are usually sky high. The advice I am about to give will mean a little bit of inconvenience, but it will be worth it. This may not work in the western United States, but in the majority of the country is will. Fly to a bigger city and drive the rest of the way. The airfare will almost certainly be cheaper. That however, is not the reason I suggest avoiding flying into smaller cities. If there is bad weather in that small town, then there is a possibility that the flight will be cancelled. If it were a bigger city or an airline hub, the odds of it canceling are lower. There is no guarantee that a bigger city flight won't cancel but it is less likely than one to a smaller town. If the plane is delayed or canceled for any reason, there are most likely very few options to rebook you on a competing airline. That means your main option is to wait. Which can sometimes mean a few days until you can get a flight. You may also be forced to drive to another city yourself. If it is weather related, you will be paying for your hotel if you are waiting for the next flight. You'll also be paying for your rental car, if you choose to drive to another city. Avoid the possible headache and just fly to bigger cities.

#136

Take The First Flight Out

Whenever possible, take the first flight out of a city in the morning. At that point, there should be very few delays, even if there is bad weather in your destination. If there are delays, since you're one of the first ones out, you will be on the top of the list to be cleared to head to your destination. The flight may sometimes have a crew rest delay, but those are less common now than they were in the past. The plane won't be affected by delays stacking up like they would be if you took a flight in the afternoon or early evening. If you are somehow delayed and miss your connection, there are usually more flights available to rebook you on. If it isn't possible to rebook you directly on your connection. There are many more options they can use to get you where you need to go. Morning flights are usually more peaceful as well. Passengers are tired and many go back to sleep. Babies and children are tired and fall asleep a lot of the time. The cabin is usually very quiet, especially if we take off before sunrise. A lot of times I'll work a morning flight from Key West. Those passengers are usually very tired or hung over and most only want water to drink. It is a very pleasant experience for both passengers and crew. I once had a flight out of Lincoln, Nebraska where we hit a flock of geese on takeoff. It resulted in us losing an engine. It was still dark out, so most passengers were asleep. The plane got rocked pretty hard. The passengers in the front few rows could hear the warning sounds through the Flight Deck door like I could. The majority of the plane was asleep, and one person didn't even know we had made an emergency landing. I had to wake him up so he could deplane. Since it was early, they were able to rebook all the passengers to get to their destinations relatively easily. If that had happened on a late afternoon or early evening flight, most of the passengers would have had to spend the night. The early bird gets the worm, but the early passenger is better prepared for unforeseen issues that can affect getting to their destination.

#137

The Flight Attendant Didn't Miss You

One of the most annoying things for Flight Attendants is when a sleeping passenger wakes up and insists you missed them while serving. We did not miss you. You were sleeping. I have seen newer Flight Attendants wake up sleeping passengers for the beverage service and have gotten yelled at. That's why most of us let sleeping passengers sleep. If we notice that they have woken up, we ask if they would like something. If we don't ask, the passenger is free to ring their call light. It never fails, the sleeping passenger will inform us that we missed them. I try my best to contain my facial expressions from this false statement. A friend has informed me that I don't do that very well. Some passengers may have picked up on my annoyance. It seems that a lot of the sleepers wake up once you are a row or two past them. You can see them out of the corner of your eye looking at you, hoping that you will notice them. Sometimes if you are close, you can ask them, but often times you are several rows away. They almost never say anything to you. It is more efficient to ask them on your way back to the galley. I know of one Flight Attendant who is especially irritated by pretty much anything passenger related. He likes to play a little game. He will notice Rip van Passenger wake up out of the corner of his eye a few rows away. He will keep looking back as he moves his way through the cabin. On his way back to the galley, he will see the sparkle in their eyes like a dog wagging its tail expecting a treat. About 2 rows away from the passenger, he will switch hands and turn away while he pulls the cart, thus giving the passenger his back. Around 2 rows away from the other side of the passenger, he will turn back around and see them looking crestfallen. He will quickly stow the beverage cart and then grab a trash bag to go through the cabin collecting trash. Before the passenger says anything, he says that they were asleep when he came by. He asks if they would like anything. The passenger is so happy and will thank him several times. The Flight Attendant is a villain but becomes the hero. Most of us aren't like him, but we do get frustrated with being told we missed people who were sleeping. Next time, admit that you were asleep and not accuse us of missing you. You might even get an appreciative smile.

#138

Be A Courteous Shopper

This is one of those things where you receive no benefit for doing it, nor would the world be a terrible place if you didn't. When I am grocery shopping, sometimes an item is at the back of the shelf. I will pull it forward for the next customer. A lot of shoppers are elderly, and this helps them out. I especially do it on top and bottom shelves where it may be hard to see the items pushed way back. Stores have grocery stockers that make the shelves look nice. Unfortunately, a lot of the stockers are young and don't pay attention. They will often cover over an item with something else because they didn't pull the products forward. It may cause someone else to think they are out of an item because they cannot see it. I guess once a grocery stocker, always a grocery stocker. When I am shopping, it takes me back to the late 90s and my first job in a grocery store. I still find myself thinking about customers even though they aren't my customer. It isn't hard to take two seconds and pull products forward. I am sure a little old lady will be glad you did.

#139

Raise Those Below You Up, Don't Push Them Down

In criminal organizations, the boss often fears those below them because of the risk of them trying to takeover. It shouldn't be that way in a corporation. I have experienced that firsthand for over a decade. I know the industry well. I know our competitors as well as possible challenges and opportunities. I have gotten both a Bachelor's and Master's in business. I have applied countless times for positions that I am both qualified and overqualified for. I have applied for special assignment opportunities as well. One time, the person who was hiring told me that the person at the top of the department told them not to pick me. It is not a surprise. Weak people fear strength and people who are educated. They see them as a threat and not an asset who can help the company. I have always said that they hire and promote based on compliance and not competence. If you look at the people they have promoted, they have surrounded themselves with ineptitude and servitude. I have complained to their bosses several times over the years. One CEO even met with me to hear my issues. He was surprised when I handed him a 31-page report that I had created showing both problems and how to fix them. I also included ways to save around $5-7 million. I know it was read by my department heads because some of my suggestions were implemented. The CEO said the issue was that my boss was threatened by me because of my intellect. They see me as a threat to their power. That was not a surprise. Leaders lead and managers manage. A leader welcomes suggestions and a manager fears them. They see any new ideas or passionate employees as a threat. Deep down, they know they are in a position where they are not the best person for the job. They know that someday someone will see that and replace them. They live in constant fear they will be exposed. Don't be like them. Be a leader who seeks to take new ideas and people and make your company a better place. Your employees will thank you and work even harder for you.

#140

Be Who You Are, Not Who They Say You Are

People like to give labels to other people. It could be good or in most cases they are bad. It may be someone they don't like or understand. I know this well. I am honest sometimes brutally. Many people cannot handle that and get upset. I am told that I am mean, even though what I said wasn't mean at all. They create this false persona of a bully even though bullying did not occur. They tell others and before you know it, you're known as something you are not. I had someone tell me after a day of flying together that they were scared to fly with me. They said someone who had never met me told them they thought I was mean from Facebook. She said that they were wrong, and that I was actually very nice. I thanked her and said I thought it was funny that she waited for a full day before being sure. She laughed. I will not allow people to label me. I will be me and I will not change. I am not going to allow people's misunderstandings or biases shape other's opinions of me. I will always stand up for what is right, even if I don't necessarily like you. I have found people to be very surprised when I have stood up for them, after they spoke ill of me. If you want to know who I am, meet the person not the legend. You will find the real me is not what you've been told. I encourage you to let others know the real you as well.

146

#141

Try To Understand The Why

The world has become far too busy. We often accept how things are and never try to understand or seek out the why. One flight the captain made a pa that we would be returning to Memphis. A passenger got very angry and upset. She was rather rude and told me we needed to continue to Gulfport. I took a moment to ask why. She told me that the airline had caused her to miss her first flight because of her connection being late. She was on her way to her grandson's funeral and because we were returning to Memphis, she would be missing it. After hearing that you couldn't help but be sad for her. Without finding out the why, she would have just seemed like an angry customer. There are many situations in life where asking why can help you understand people and their behavior. You can avoid conflict or help someone out. It takes very little effort to care enough to ask why. You will never know what you can do, if you just ask why. It seems like no one wants to cut through the emotion and listen to find out the why. Those few seconds can save you a lot of time dealing with people both on a personal and professional level. You can defuse a situation more easily when you understand the why. It shows that you care and will help you be more empathetic. So, ask why.

#142

Don't Be A Tattle Tale

In life and especially work, there are moments where reporting to superiors is required. If someone is committing a crime or is being unsafe. They may be acting as a danger to themselves or others. Those moments need to be reported ASAP. There are other moments where people feel the need to be a tattletale. It might be something small that the other person doesn't even know is against the rules. I give people that I fly with a briefing of the rules of flying with me. I tell that them if I see something that could get them in trouble. I will let them know. It is up to them if they choose to change or not. Often times, if I tell them what I observed they had no clue that what they were doing could get them in trouble. They thank me for letting them know. Some people would just write them up without taking the time to talk it over with them. It could be a teachable moment. I have found that the biggest tattletales are people who are in trouble themselves. For whatever reason, they think telling on their coworkers will help them. It never does. It actually expedites them getting fired. They get a reputation as someone who is a tattletale. Their coworkers watch them like a hawk and write them up. Instead of laying low, they paint a giant target on their own back. The company finds out about the issues they are creating. Then poof, they're nothing but a memory. Don't be like them. Don't tattle. Educate those who need help.

#143

It's Not A Small Plane

Stop complaining about the size of the plane when you board. You are more than likely flying to an airport with less than 10 gates. It does not necessitate a big plane. It never fails, people will board and say, "Oh my gosh, this plane is so small". I will often make jokes about how we are flying to Des Moines not Paris. Sometimes I will act offended and say, "hey now, we have two bathrooms". We didn't pick the size of the plane that is flying to your destination. Please send your aircraft size complaints to someone further up the food chain. While you are at it, see if you can get me a raise. Thanks. If given the choice, I would prefer not to fly to whatever winter wonderland or swampland in the dead heat of summer, we are headed to. Most regional flights don't go anywhere exciting or desirable. I apologize to all the towns who are now offended.

#144

It Fit On The Last Plane

Regional jets have smaller overhead bins than larger planes. That means a lot of roller bags that fit on a 737 will not fit on our plane. That is why the gate agent gives out special tags to put on your bag. You leave it on the jetbridge or a luggage cart as you board. You will receive it at your arrival city on the jetbridge or a luggage cart. Unless of course, the ramp agents in your arrival city are lazy and send them all to baggage claim with the checked luggage. That's a whole other rant that I will not get into. There are many passengers who are certain that their bag will fit. They will argue with the Flight Attendant who insists that they gate check it. They will always utter the same phrase, "it fit on the last plane". I am sure it did, but it will probably not on this one. In 19 years, I have not had a fight with a passenger over bags because of one reason. I give them the information and don't fight them. I tell them that I don't think it will fit but I allow them the opportunity to let them try. The majority of the time they will give up their bag without a fight. I tell them they can try but they don't want to have to bring it back up if it doesn't fit. I have had people whose bag I didn't think would fit somehow get it into the bin. Others have tried and have had to bring their bag back up to check it. Many of them thank me for letting them try. I know the probable outcome so arguing with them is pointless. I have had to represent Flight Attendants in meetings who have been written up by passengers. The problem with the passenger almost always starts with them having an argument about checking their bag. If your first encounter is getting the customer angry, it will only go downhill from there. Flight Attendants, let them try. Passengers, accept it might not fit and get your keys, medicines and valuables out before you gate check your bag.

#145

Know How To Evacuate

Passengers rarely pay attention to the safety demonstration. I will admit after having to do it over 10,000 times it is very boring. You will more than likely not need to know how to evacuate. However, there is a chance that one time you may need to know. The vast majority of people who have flown know how to use a seatbelt and oxygen mask. What you need to know is where your nearest exit is and how to use it. That knowledge can be the difference between living and dying in an emergency. Read your safety card. Know if the aircraft you are on has life vests or if you will need to use seat cushions in a water landing. Count how many rows you are from your first exit choice and also your second choice. In a smoky cabin, you might not be able to see the exit, but you can count how many seatbacks you are away from the exit and find your way out. Take note of your fellow passengers to see if there are children, elderly or disabled passengers who may need your help. You cannot rely on the Flight Attendants being able to help you. They may be incapacitated or unable to help. Your survival depends on you. Most importantly, leave your luggage behind. The time it takes to get your bag could cause someone else to not be able to evacuate. Your luggage isn't more valuable than a human life. As evidenced recently in Tokyo, there is not a lot of time before the entire aircraft is engulfed in flames. Every second counts. Educate yourself, so that you are prepared if you need to evacuate.

#146

Don't Live Life Like A Movie

Romantic comedies often have moments where the man realizes he can't live without the woman. He runs to catch a train or hurries to the airport, violates all airport security rules and catches her at her gate. We will completely ignore the fact if that happens her flight isn't going to be allowed to leave and everyone will have to be rescreened. He will also more than likely be arrested. The passengers will not find his gesture romantic and will be very angry. Anywho, back to my story. I was in London, Greenwich to be exact, on a trip with a friend. Our last night before flying home, I walked to this grocery store to pick up some British treats to take home. I vividly remember a dog being tied up outside. I walk in and there is this brunette woman checking out. She looks at me and smiles. I went to get my items. Then, I had a moment of sudden insanity come over me and decided that I needed to talk to this woman. I never watch romantic comedies so I can't blame it on that. I leave the store and head across the parking lot to the street in a full sprint. It was a long time ago when I could still run. I have no idea where this woman went, but without looking, I run right across a busy street. It was a miracle I wasn't ran over. I get about two blocks before I come to my senses. I think to myself what am I doing? What is this woman going to think? She was polite and smiled at me. She didn't profess her love to me. Thankfully, British people don't own guns, so I wouldn't get shot but possibly maced. I slow down and come to a stop. I turn around and walk back to the store to get what I went there to get. The whole time questioning what on earth I had just done. I still don't know what I was thinking. There is a small chance that woman is reading this. Sorry, but you had your chance. If you had walked slower our lives could have been the subject of a whatever the British equivalent of the Hallmark Channel is. So yeah, don't do what I did.

#147

How To Pee In Turbulence Without Getting Your Shoes Wet

The advice you have all been waiting for. It only took reading through 146 other tidbits of possibly helpful information to get here. This is both a metaphor as well as actual advice. I'll start with the real advice first. I have joked that in 19 years as a Flight Attendant, I have learned 2 life skills. I can get an overhead bin to close, and I can pee in turbulence without getting my shoes wet. People laugh, but those truly are the only two skills I have acquired. Customer service skills I already had. I may have refined them, but they were there. Those of you who sit when you pee won't find this advice to be beneficial. I pick one of the walls of the lavatory and lean against it hard and brace myself. Don't lean against the door or you might hit turbulence and give everyone a free show they might not want to see. Once I am anchored against the wall I just pee like normal. It really is pretty simple. Even in the roughest air, my shoes are pee free. Give it a try, you and your shoes will thank me. The metaphor is pretty simple as well. If you are anchored with family, friends, God or anything else that is meaningful to you. You are able to successfully navigate turbulence in life. Both are simple tips that will help you in life. Well, one will mostly help your shoes but you get my point.

#148

Take The Money

Airlines love to oversell flights. It is something that I do not understand how it is legal. Airlines are selling things that they do not actually have. I know the analysts do all the figuring, so they know that 6 people don't show up on Tuesdays on the 8pm flight to Omaha. They account for that in their sales numbers. Many times, on those oversold flights everyone shows up. The airlines then become auctioneers offering hundreds and sometimes thousands of dollars to go on a different flight. Many people will hold out hoping for a higher number. There is one instance where you should be the first one to volunteer. If the flight is delayed and it looks like you might miss your connection, then volunteer. If you miss your connection, you most likely will be paying for a hotel on your own dime. If you volunteer, you will get where you need to go and get several hundred dollars as well. You will probably get your hotel paid for was well. You won't have to worry about paying for a hotel in a city that is most likely expensive and has few hotels left. Take the money and get a better end result.

#149

Ding Only When Necessary

There are two groups when it comes to dinging the Flight Attendant call light. There are the people who are afraid to use it. Then there are the people who feel like it is the bell for their butler. They ring it for everything. Both types are wrong in their usage. The first group should ring it more. It is ok and much preferred to being poked and prodded as we walk by. We will be happy to assist you. The other group needs to ring it way less. They ring it for simple things that are not time sensitive. A lot of them will ring it as we are going down the runway or the second that we are off the ground. It is unsafe for us to come see what they need. Many times, they will be angry they had to wait and usually their request is for something like a blanket. We are not going to risk injury to ourselves and other passengers for something that can wait the 5 minutes until we are at 10,000 feet. Then it will be safe for us to get out of our jumpseat. I know some Flight Attendants will make a pa acknowledging the call light and say that if it is an emergency involving the safety of the airplane or someone is having a medical issue to ring it again. The passenger usually turns it off because they realize it can wait. I had a Flight Attendant tell me last week someone rang it again when they made that announcement. Fearing it was a medical emergency, the Flight Attendant rushed to the passenger. The passenger wanted a fork. The Flight Attendant had to explain to them that it was not an emergency. I think it is funny when people accidentally turn it on trying to turn on their reading light. They will hurriedly try to turn it off and frantically wave you off as you head to their seat. That always makes me chuckle a little. I wish that more people felt the same way about turning their light on. We will always answer the call light. We just ask that you are situationally aware and know to wait until it is safe for us to come to your seat before you ring it. Also, please only consider things to be an emergency if they actually are an emergency.

#150

Don't Wait To Board

It never fails, we are ready to go but we have to wait on one passenger. We understand people get stuck in security or are connecting from other flights. However, a lot of times people are in the bar or airline lounge and take their time to board. It helps us arrive on time if we leave on time or a little early. A lot of airline crew commute and are hurrying to catch a flight home. They will coordinate leaving early with the gate agent and ground crew. Everyone will be onboard but one person who decided to wait to board. The crew gets more annoyed when the person saunters down the jetbridge and is angry the gate agent paged them. Don't be that person. Board early and be ready to go. We appreciate that whether we tell you or not. Help us get you to your destination on time.

#151

No, This Isn't Our Route Or Home

A common question airline crew get from passengers is, "do you live (insert small town) or is this your route?' Flights are not bus routes. We do not spend all day flying back and forth from your little town to the hub. We might visit your city once a month or once a year. There is no consistency to where we fly or what flights we work. Now at mainline carriers some of the very senior (knew Orville and Wilbur level senior) can pick to only fly to certain international cities. Regional crews cannot. We would probably go insane if all we ever did were trips to somewhere like (insert random small town so no city is mad at me). We also do not live in the cities we fly to. A very small number of crews do but the majority do not. Most live in the hub cities or commute to somewhere else. Pilots usually live somewhere in Florida it seems. Once someone didn't like how I said no when they asked if I lived in their city. Apparently, they thought my no was offensive. If that offended them, I am glad they didn't ask the reasons why. Depending upon the city, I may have a very lengthy list of reasons why I don't want to live in (insert small town). In the future, do not ask either of those two things. I will now silently thank you for your future good deeds.

#152

Unions Can Sometimes Be Useful

It seems that in America, you are either 100% a diehard unionist or anti-union. There seems to be very few folks in between. I am one of the few. I believe in certain industries and companies a union is a necessity. The airline industry is one of those industries. However, not all airlines are or seem to need to be unionized. One of the biggest airlines has almost an entirely non-union work force. That seems to work for them because only one of the work groups has chosen to be unionized in recent attempts to unionize all of them. One of the biggest obstacles to effective union representation in the airline industry is the Railway Labor Act. It is an antiquated Act of Congress that makes it almost impossible to strike. It was created for railroads to ensure small towns received supplies and people were able to travel. The world is a very different place now, so the Act really is unnecessary. Airlines love it because it makes negotiating easier because unions do not have the threat of a quick strike like the autoworkers recently did. Airline workers have to jump through so many hoops to be able to strike. That really hurts a union's effectiveness. Another issue are the unions themselves. Some airlines don't unionize because how the unions themselves behave. Unions are a business. They don't like the comparison, but it is accurate. They want and need members' dues to survive. That is why they will concentrate their efforts to organize as many companies as possible. They try to portray it as helping those workers but at the end of the day, it is the millions of dollars of potential dues that motivates them. Some union officers then use those dues to ensure they don't have to work. They are supposedly volunteers, but they use union money to pay for their days off. I have no problem with people being compensated because the amount of time that is spent doing the positions. I have issue with how people use their paid union days off to work the system, so that they almost never have to work. Then there are the internal systems designed to "protect" the union. Members can petition to have a vote to recall an officer they feel is not adequately representing them. However, in some instances, the decision to allow the petition is decided by the offending officer's equals. It is reasonable to believe they could face a similar situation. A logical person could see that it is not in their personal best interest to allow the petition because of that. Plus, in some circumstances officers could band together to protect each other and avoid being held accountable. Those are some of the reasons people don't trust unions. There is also no system to hold officers accountable who choose to attack their fellow officers. There is a system that is abused to put an officer up on charges. An officer's fate is decided by officers many of whom may be friends with the person filing the charges. It is a corrupt system that does not help the members whose interests are supposed to come first. It is a system, where one hate filled person can sabotage their fellow officers and is not one that is beneficial to the people whose money they take. The charges could not even be legitimate but because of the system and those deciding fates, innocent people could be harmed. If you want to be non-union because your situation is working more power to you. If you are a company that wants to remain non-union, listen to your workers concerns. As long as you address the issues and treat your workers fairly, they will never unionize. My Grandfather was a non-union factory worker. His company treated their employees like kings. They gave huge profit-sharing checks and you had to know someone who worked there just to get an interview. The family who owned it sold the company. The new owners did not understand the reason for the company's success was how they treated their employees. The quality and sales have suffered greatly. It has greatly hurt the company's reputation and you no longer need to know anyone to get an interview. If you want to unionize your company, make sure you research the various union options. One may promise you the world and deliver much, much less. Talk to people who are currently represented by that union so you can get an honest opinion of how things really are. Talk to normal workers not union officers. Officers will give you biased information to sway you. To the unions out there I say this: you hold onto the past glories of unionism. You made great progress for workers and then you got complacent. You haven't lived up to the standards of your predecessors. We no longer are at risk of 80-hour work weeks in unsafe conditions or having 9-year-olds working in slaughterhouses. The unions of the past would be ashamed to be compared to you. Do better, be better and purge those who are only in it for themselves and the perceived power they get from their position. Based upon how you always react to calls to change defensively, this will be seen and reported as an attack. It isn't and you know that but because you don't want to change, I am made the villain. A union's greatest enemy lives in the mirrors above the sinks of union officers. Look within yourselves, embrace criticism as changes that need to be made to ensure the union's survival and honoring those who fought for workers before.

#153

Don't Be A Job Dinosaur

In many jobs, especially in the airline industry there are job dinosaurs. People who have worked for several decades but don't retire. In many cases, they know they don't have the ability to do their entire job. They usually have a bad attitude and are rude to customers and coworkers alike. They keep working for a variety of reasons. There are two main reasons. One being that they are at the top of the payscale, so they make a lot of money. The other being that they don't know what else to do. Their life has been that job for years, so they don't know how to do anything else. The job has become their identity so they would lose their identity and self-worth if they didn't get to brag about their job and places they get to go. Many airlines are worried about being sued for age discrimination, so the very senior Flight Attendants experience this level of protection not afforded to younger Flight Attendants. It is almost similar to tenure at a college. There was a Flight Attendant who was the oldest Flight Attendant in the industry. They were in their early 90s. They could not do 100% of their duties but was still allowed to fly. I know people who flew with them and said they would do very little on the plane because they knew they didn't have to. The funny thing is that they hated their company. They allegedly flew with a suit in their luggage because they hoped to die on a layover and the company would have to pay to ship their body back home. Every year, Flight Attendants are required to attend annual training and testing to prove that they can still do their job, as well as have the knowledge necessary to do the job. At one airline, a very senior group of Flight Attendants would bring along a lawyer to intimidate the company into passing them. At another airline, an FAA inspector observed a Flight Attendant take a luggage cart and use it as a walker on the way to their flight. The FAA inspector made her go back and walk without it to the gate and she could not. She had recently passed annual training. The FAA allegedly made her go back to the training center and do it with them observing. She could not do it. Most of these Flight Attendants know they cannot perform all their duties that would be required in an emergency. Instead of doing the honorable thing and retiring, they fight to keep their jobs. They cannot fathom the idea of no longer having their identity. Their behavior is nothing short of selfishness and narcissism. They put passengers, their coworkers and themselves at risk. Do the right thing and retire. You've had a good career. Don't risk ending it with someone dying because you hung on too long.

#154

Your Job Isn't That Important

Humans like to feel important, so they often inflate their importance for their ego. One of the biggest offenders of that are Flight Attendants. There has been this push to call us First Responders. I and others not only disagree with that comparison, but also feel very uncomfortable with lumping us in with police, fire and medical professionals. The speech that often accompanies the inaccurate comparison is that Flight Attendants were the first on the scene on 9/11. That makes it seem that the passengers were not there as well. First Responders jobs are inherently dangerous, and their roles can be the difference between life or death to the people they serve on a daily basis. Flight Attendants can have a several decade career without someone else's life being at risk. It is insulting to the real First Responders who they are comparing themselves to. During the pandemic, McDonald's was giving away value meals to First Responders to say thank you. Several Flight Attendants went to get one and some even bragged about fighting with McDonald's to get one. That is disgusting and embarrassing. To the real First Responders I say thank you. I am sorry my compatriots feel the need to dishonor your jobs and compare themselves undeservedly to you. I've never saved someone's life with a Coke and a cookie. We are trained to handle an emergency. We don't deal with them on a daily basis. The recent crash in Tokyo has caused many Flight Attendants to go crazy on the over importance of Flight Attendants. One meme that many Flight Attendants have shared, said that if the pilots, air traffic control and maintenance fail that the Flight Attendants are here to save everyone. It is infuriating how foolish and wrong that mentality is. We are all a team and to claim that somehow, we are these superheroes is wrong. Please have some decency and stop calling Flight Attendants First Responders.

#155

Stop Hitting On FAs

As a fat, bald, straight white guy in his late 30sish, this is not something I have ever had to deal with. Apparently, Flight Attendants get hit on, a lot. I have had coworkers tell me how they will frequently get hit on by passengers. From comments to business cards to attempts to be creative at note writing they have seen it all. I know a few people who have had relationships start from meeting on a plane. I know of a former coworker who has a baby from a passenger they met on a flight. They supposedly dated first, so it isn't as scandalous, but it all started with a flight. I know it gets tiring for these Flight Attendants both men and women. It seems like pretty much everyone is getting hit on but me while working flights. Lol. You aren't creative so please stop. I can guarantee almost 99% of the time whatever you handed the Flight Attendant is in the trash before they make you put your tray tables up for landing. Don't do it. You look desperate and pathetic. People deserve to go to work without being hit on. Once a passenger handed a note to a Flight Attendant I was working with. We joked that I should go back and thank him for the note and say I'd call him. We decided I would somehow end up in an HR meeting and aborted my mission. Your flight is there to get you to your destination. Stow your love life aspirations at the door.

#156

Pilots Are Thrifty

Pilots are some of the wealthiest and cheapest people you will ever meet. The things I have observed or have heard about are crazy. The old Indianapolis airport had a food court where for some reason all the restaurants would give samples. I knew a pilot who would go get a sample from each restaurant. Then he would take his suit coat off and go through again. Then he would put on a non-uniform coat and go through a third time. He would say he got a full meal that way. There are also pilots who would keep paper cups so they could get free refills from coffee places in the airports that gave refills. Once, I was in line in the Memphis Airport for Lenny's Subs. This pilot turns around to tell me to order the Kids Meal. He said that it is cheaper than a sub by itself and you get chips, a drink and a cookie. I think that location probably set the record for the most kids meals sold. There was a pilot who when florescent light bulbs were more expensive would allegedly bring burned out regular bulbs from home. I don't know if that was an urban legend but based on my knowledge of pilots it is believable. Pilots and Flight Attendants will often sleep in recliners in the crew room to save money. This one pilot from a mainline carrier told me how he often takes a nap in the La Guardia Airport crew room. He then wakes up and walks across the street to the Marriott. He said when housekeeping checks rooms, they flip the safety latch, so the door doesn't close. That way they know which rooms are empty and available to be cleaned. He said that he goes into one of those rooms and puts the do not disturb sign out. He said if he is lucky, it is a 2 bed room and one of the beds wasn't slept in. He takes a nap and wakes up to take a shower. He was very proud to tell a random stranger his little scam. Pilots are also obsessed with getting food for free. They will rave about a crappy breakfast at a hotel because it is free. I had one argue with me in the hotel van because he thought it was so good. Spoiler alert: it was not. They will scavenge bins in the galley looking for food like raccoons. They will rip open first-class snack baskets for food they want to eat. They are the worst when it comes to first class meals. I have had pilots ask if there will be extra meals before the passengers even board. They will call up in the middle of service to bug Flight

Attendants about leftover meals. It is beyond annoying that people who make so much money are so cheap and interfere with your duties. One guy always asks what there is and says, "I'll take a look at it". He acts like somehow; he is doing us a favor by taking the extra meal. Sorry sir, but you are not doing me a favor. Your cheapness is wasting my time. Some Flight Attendants get upset when pilots don't buy them food or coffee. I don't expect them to buy me anything as their money is their money. I am always appreciative when they buy me something even as small as a Dr. Pepper. Some are generous but sadly those are few and far between. It is ironic, because when I started. Regional pilots were often on food stamps. When they upgraded to captain, they would often buy dinner. Now it seems that as regional pilots are well paid, they have gotten even cheaper especially when it comes to scavenging food off the airplane.

#157

Regional Flight Attendants Are Poor

There is this common misconception that Flight Attendants make a livable wage. At the mainline airline level that is true. At the regional level that couldn't be further from the truth. People see the pay scale and think $24 an hour makes as much as a full time 9-5 job which would be $48,000. The reality is airline pay is equal to about half that, so $24 an hour is like working a job making $12 an hour. You also have the added costs of food while you travel. You get per diem but that doesn't cover the cost of expensive airport meals. When I started, I made $15 an hour which is like making $7.50 an hour. It was a struggle and after 19 years still is. After 19 years, I make around $40,000. If I worked for a mainline carrier, it would be almost double that. The line airlines like to use is, "you are a regional flight attendant". It has been used for several years to justify the poverty wages. The FAA mandates 1 Flight Attendant per 50 passengers. It is no different for a 777 than a 50 seat CRJ 200. Airlines have been making record profits while regional Flight Attendants starve. I have received numerous emails from Flight Attendants sharing their stories. Many are based in one of the most expensive places in the U.S., New York City. They make less than minimum wage for NYC. One Flight Attendant shared the heartbreaking story of having to put milk back at the grocery store because she couldn't afford it. Her story got even more upsetting when she shared that she couldn't afford a birthday cake for her son. I know of people who have basically lived in the airport crew room because they couldn't afford rent. I know people who eat as much free breakfast and free meals in the crew room as they can because they can't afford to eat. This is while the mainline carriers they fly for make billions in profits. There are a good portion of regional Flight Attendants on some form of government assistance. Airlines to my knowledge do not pay taxes on baggage fees. They make profits with wages that cause an increase in citizens on government assistance, but don't pay taxes on a large portion of those profits. They are robbing the American taxpayer twice. The next time you are on a regional flight your Flight Attendant might have slept in a recliner or the only meal they've had has been cookies on the airplane. They will provide the best service they can while struggling to survive. The airline will tell you how much your business matters, but the question is, why do the people who help make those billions in profit not matter enough to be paid enough to live?

#158

Don't Get In The Drama

Everyone loves the tea as young people call gossip. However, getting in the middle of drama is never advised. It is best to stay away or say things like "that's crazy", "Wow" or anything else that makes them think you support them but can't be used against you as taking a side. I made the mistake of getting into drama at an office job I had. There was a young single mom whose mom was some sort of manager in the company. There was a young mom who was married. The single mom hated the married mom. There was a lot of tension in the office. I had to be trained by the single mom on something. She was very helpful. I made the joke that the married mom was wrong and that she wasn't so bad after all. She got angry and asked what she said. I said that she hadn't said anything and that I was joking. She didn't believe me and reported the situation to Human Resources. I ended up getting called into a meeting and since I was on probation I was fired. I can say fired unlike everyone else who seem to say something else like, "I was let go" or some other phrase to make it sound not as bad. That prepared me for being a Flight Attendant as I knew to steer clear of the drama. Thankfully, I work with one other Flight Attendant at a time so the potential for drama is lower but still exists. People tell me how they don't like someone and expect me to join their side. When in reality, I have no issue with their enemy. I have had Flight Attendants ask me to ask the Flight Attendant that I was working with why they didn't answer their messages on a dating app. I politely said, "Ummm, no". Flight Attendants are the most drama filled work group in any job. Sometimes passengers can even pick up on the tension. I suggest that you do as I do and avoid the drama. Unless you like drama, then once you get them started. You won't get them to stop sharing everything about everyone that they have an issue with. It could be the other Flight Attendant, a Pilot or the guy in 7C. They will make sure you know why they are mad at them. Just make sure you don't become part of their drama.

#159

Disagreeing Isn't Bullying

Bullying is bad. However, not all situations are bullying. I know someone who whenever they are losing an argument will cry bullying. There is absolutely no evidence to support their claim. They think by saying that they are being bullied. Other people will jump in and stop the other person. Most of the time it involves this person being held accountable for shady things they do or say. They will add people into an email chain and cry bullying like the boy who cried wolf. Not once has any of the people they tagged in, stepped up to support their claims of bullying. It really is not only a sign of weakness but of being manipulative. People are scared of being called names like bully so they will often back down. They could be completely in the right but will succumb to the manipulation. I know what is and is not bullying. I am not a bully, nor will I allow someone to manipulate people into believing I am one. I will not back down especially when the facts support me attempting to hold them accountable. I suggest that those of you who cry fake bullying take a moment for self-reflection and choose to not continue your manipulative path. You are being harmful to the victims of real bullying. Those of you who are victims of fake claims of bullying I urge you to stay strong. You are not a bully. Let the truth support you and know that you are right no matter the lies, distortion, and desperate attempts to undermine you. Those of you who are actual bullies just stop. You are weak and bully people out of weakness.

#160

Blocking Is Lame

I think one of the lamest things you can do on social media is block people. I understand there are safety reasons for blocking and I 100% support those. I know people who have had strangers message them to say their children are cute. That is just creepy and potentially a safety risk. Block those creeps ASAP!! I know people who have coworkers who take screenshots and turn them into their employer. It's totally cool to block them. You may have a sibling who reports everything you say or post to your parents. Go ahead and block them too. What I am referring to are the people who disagree with you, and then you block them. I have had someone say something as a joke that was offensive to a family member of mine. I confronted them about it, and they blocked me. They were in the wrong but felt the need to block me. Then there are the partisans. "If you support (insert politician) you might as well unfriend me now." The world works with different viewpoints. If you don't like Aunt Carol's memes supporting Trump, just unfollow her. There is no need to block her. We were once a nation that welcomed different beliefs on issues. Now it seems we have two sides and that is it. So, stop your blocking of people who you call friends or relatives. It is very closed minded and intolerant. You don't have to agree with them. It is not hard to be civil, agree to disagree and scroll on. No need to start a fight in the comments or block them.

#161

Exit Row Lies

Before every flight we are required to brief the passengers sitting in the exit row. We inform them that they are in the exit row and ask if they are ready, willing and able to assist in an emergency. They are supposed to read the card in the seat back and confirm that they are able to perform the duties. There are restrictions, for instance: you cannot use a seat belt extension, although I have been told that rule is supposedly airline specific. You cannot be disabled and need to be able to lift the 35-pound window and take it out to open it. In 19 years, I have had less than 5 people tell me that they don't believe they can fulfill the duties. They are always very apologetic. I reassure them they did the right thing and thank them for thinking of others. It is pretty easy to find someone willing to trade seats for the extra legroom. The annoying thing is that when we brief the exit row, and they say they can perform the duties we have to accept that. Even if we feel that one of them would not be able to open the window. We have to accept their yes as they are able to do it. There has been a high number of people that I believe would not be able to open the window. I am sure they know it as well. They lie so that they can get some extra legroom. I have had several elderly women who struggled to carry their purses tell me they could open the window. It is a safety risk to allow these people to continue to lie. They put everyone at risk with their selfishness. This needs to change but until the FAA acts it is up to the passengers to be honest and put everyone else's safety first. Don't let your legroom greed be the reason someone doesn't survive if we have to evacuate the airplane.

#162

Perception Is Everything

The truth matters most of all. However, one thing that is often overlooked is perception. Often times, perception can be more important than reality. In working as a Flight Attendant for 19 years, I have had to deal with perception in many different ways. Flight Attendants have often relied on perception whether through hearing gossip or not researching an issue for the truth. They believe what they perceive to be true. It is especially true when it comes to contract voting. They often hear something about the proposed contract and parrot that to their friends and coworkers. It might not be true, but it is their perception about the agreement. Companies love that because they can wage a PR campaign and people won't research before they vote. In an effort to combat that and educate my coworkers I created a podcast several years ago about a contract we were voting on. I simply explained the changes and their effects both positive and negative. I did not tell anyone how to vote. I simply explained things for people who did not understand. Many people thanked me for explaining it clearly. It caused many people to be vocally opposed to it. A member of management was not liking how my education campaign was possibly changing the outcome of the vote. They decided to publicly slander me. Flight Attendants were required to attend an event where they were told how great they were and in the second half told how much better they needed to be at their job. Most people hated it. Allegedly out of nowhere, this member of management decided to tell all the Flight Attendants gathered not to listen to my podcast. They said it was full of false and misleading information. That was a complete lie. It happened for sure at one event, but I had heard possibly at another event or two. They then said that they were the only source of correct information. I emailed that manager asking what information I had incorrect and that if anything was incorrect, I would issue a correction. The fact I never received any information or a response at all showed that there was no false information, but they were trying to manipulate perception. The funny thing is that I wasn't telling anyone how to vote. I was just explaining the changes and their effects.

Another time, I was on a flight where we were overweight and needed to remove 6 passengers. I had to walk through the cabin and tell 6 passengers that they had to get off the aircraft. This passenger in the back of the cabin rang her call light and was very angry. She asked me why I was removing people off the plane. I said we were overweight and that we needed to have 6 less people. She didn't seem to like this response and was still angry. She asked why I picked those people. I stopped for a second and realized that from her point of the view what her perception was. I was a white guy walking through the cabin and seemingly picking random nonwhite people to remove from the plane. I explained to her that they were employees traveling for free and that free passengers get removed before taking off paying passengers. Once I explained that, her whole demeanor changed. She actually seemed quite happy I was booting them off. I said, "I am sure it looked like I was just picking random people." She said that is how it looked but that now she understood why I picked them. I always try think of how the things I do on the plane will be perceived by people of different backgrounds or who do not have full knowledge of what is actually going on. That is something that can be helpful to do in any job or situation. If you understand how things will be perceived you can avoid a lot of problems and misunderstandings.

#163

Don't Trust Background Checks

In this country, there is this overwhelming reliance on background checks. If someone is involved in a horrible crime often involving children there is always a mention of how they passed a background check. Background checks offer a false sense of security. All that means is they haven't been caught before. I am sure almost all of the Catholic priests who abused children for decades would have passed background checks. I think in positions of trust especially involving children or the vulnerable need some sort of psychiatric evaluation. That is not my expertise, but I am sure with our advancements in technology there could be some sort of test. One that could create a risk assessment of whether that person is a danger. As with all tests, there will be people who will try and create a way to beat the test. There will probably be like in all tests, the occasional false positives for being a risk. I am sure most people would rather risk the occasional innocent person being flagged as a risk than not having the testing at all. It certainly would not replace background checks but would work in tandem. There will undoubtedly be the civil liberties people who will be opposed. While civil liberties are important these jobs most often are optional. No one makes you apply for these jobs. It seems the civil liberties people are often more concerned with the rights and feelings of the potential perpetrator and not the potential victims put at risk. I just feel that there needs to be an additional layer of safety when putting people in positions of trust. When background checks are only good for those who reoffend, there needs to be away so there is a reduced chance of a first offense. That is something I am sure most people would agree would be a good thing.

#164

Don't Lose Your Clothes In The Woods

There was a pilot and a flight attendant who decided to have some fun on a layover. Allegedly, they were drinking and ended up in the woods. Clothes were removed and things allegedly transpired. Afterwards, they could not find their clothing. They looked and looked and still could not find them. I have always been curious what exactly happened to cause them to be so far from their clothing. They wandered the woods and somehow ended up in the driveway, at I believe a fire chief's house. They broke into his vehicle and stole a flashlight to look for their clothing. I am assuming the fire chief was the person who called the police, but they were apprehended. The pilot was found wearing only a wristwatch and flip flops. They made national news and were the victim of jokes on all the late-night shows. I remember getting calls and texts from people not in the industry. That is one thing about working for an airline. If your airline makes the news, all the non-airline people you know will call, text, email, carrier pigeon asking first, if you know the person and then asking for any details that didn't make the news. They were surprisingly not fired. I had flown with that pilot and had my own interesting experience although we kept our clothes on and there was not anything similar to the alleged activities that took place in the woods. There are things that happen that get you automatically fired and there are things where alcohol is blamed. Crewmembers get sent to programs that "reform" them and they are welcomed back with a short leash. I should be clear that anything that puts passengers and fellow crewmembers at risk is never tolerated and you will not be given a second chance. I remember about 5 years later; I was using a crew room computer and saw the badge of the pilot standing next to me. It was Mr. Flipflops, but his demeanor was significantly changed. He was much more reserved. I commend him for making the necessary changes in his life. I guess the point of this is don't get naked outdoors. If you must, don't lose your clothes. Or you may make the news and become the butt of many many jokes.

#165

Cancel Cancelling

We live in the greatest age of intolerance. The majority of my life, intolerance consisted of people who treated people poorly of different races, genders, orientations and beliefs. Now, the intolerant people are everywhere. They are intolerant of anything they don't like. The irony is that they think they are the good guys. They attack and attack until they bully people into believing how they believe. They will resort to posting addresses, email addresses and phone numbers of people they disagree with. They seek to destroy anyone who they don't like or thinks differently than they do. It is beyond evil, and it is being done in the name of doing the right thing. It is people on both ends of the political spectrum who do this. They seek to cancel a person and ruin their lives. Internet allows a certain degree of anonymity and people also have keyboard courage. They say and do things they would never say or do in the presence of that person. Sometimes they lurk in the shadows and other times they love the attention they receive riling people up to agree with their stance. I personally know someone who has been partially canceled. This person is a friend who is not as close as we once were. I will be completely honest and say they have always been very intolerant of other viewpoints. To the point they will berate people and question their intelligence if their opinion is different. They were a very public figure and on their Facebook page they posted something, and I asked a simple question. They responded and attacked me, called me something that I was not and still am not, questioned my intelligence and berated my job. Strangers joined in on attacking me. It was wrong to do to anyone, much less someone who you had been friends with for almost 20 years at the time. I sent them a message. I said that you don't treat your friends that way and certainly not when they only asked a question. A question someone else later answered for me. My question wasn't controversial at all. I just was asking to understand something. If anyone deserved being canceled, it was them. A few years later, they made the news for a controversial Facebook post. In their typical angry fashion, they posted emotionally, and their post was inflammatory. Apparently, it was the second time that they had been in trouble for this type of behavior.

As their employer is out in the public and has customers of all political views they were terminated after a big push to cancel them. As someone who had been the victim of them publicly insulting and attacking me. I had a right to be mad at them. I could have felt vindicated they were held accountable by them losing their job and the campaign to cancel them. Instead, I made a post saying that while I find what they said offensive. They are my friend and that I didn't agree with canceling them. They texted me thanking me for the message, which I assume was sent to them as I had unfriended them after they bashed me. I texted their siblings and said that while that person is a jerk, they are our jerk. Humans say and do things we shouldn't and eventually end up regretting. Unless it involves a crime, there is no need to cancel people. We have freedom of speech. That is the freedom to say things good, bad or stupid. Not everyone will agree with us on everything. I have friends who I agree with on some issues but are the polar opposite on others. What the cancel people don't understand is that while today you are on the offensive to cancel someone. The day may come where you are the one being canceled. Agreeing to disagree on some issues and coming together on ones where we agree is what helped make this country great and more importantly functional. We need to get back to that. We need to end the cancel culture.

#166
Internet Dates Can Get You Killed

If you have internet dated, you have stories, I'm sure. Usually, it is women who have the stories. The guy didn't look like his picture. The guy was creepy or some other major red flag. Many people somehow do have success stories. One of the former Miss Americas met their husband on Tinder. I met my wife on Eharmony. The jury is still out on if that was a success story. It's been 15 years of marriage, so I guess in terms of marriages in this country it is considered a success. There is however one date that will forever remain in my brain and stand as an example of a really bad date. There was this Christian dating site called Love and Seek. I don't know if it still exists, but it was one of the cheaper dating sites. I chatted with a few different women over a few months, but one woman and I had a lot in common. She had family in Minnesota, and I believe she loved sports as well. She lived in Philadelphia, and I had a layover there coming up. I was getting in late at night, so she was going to pick me up in the morning. I had an afternoon flight so we would have lunch after hanging out. I got into her car, and she was cute. She asked what I wanted to do, and I said I was open to whatever. She decided we were going to see the Liberty Bell. On the drive there while she talked, I could see her cuteness was only skin deep. She was a very angry bitter person. I am like, ok this isn't going to go anywhere but I will have a good time. We park and walk towards the building housing the Liberty Bell. There are all these crowd control fences around it. There weren't many people around, so she decided to start moving fences to take a short cut. I tell her I don't think we should do that. She said it was fine. In the distance I hear yelling. I look up and see a National Park Service Ranger running towards us. He is yelling at us. He's yelling to stop. She is oblivious or just doesn't care and ignores him. He is yelling louder and getting closer. It is then I see something I will never forget. He takes his right hand as he is running and unsnaps his holster to his gun. He has his hand on his holster as he is still running. It is at this point I decide I am not going to meet my end at the hands of a National Park Service Ranger bullet. I stop following her and tell her he is yelling at us. A rational person would think, "perhaps, I am in the wrong. I shall halt my journey and assess my surroundings. I shall even ask the gentleman yelling what infraction I have committed." She did not however take his yelling as a time for thought and self-assessment. She started yelling back at him. I think to myself. "Oh great, now we are going to get shot for sure." Apparently, the Liberty Bell was closed. After they finished arguing and we didn't get shot. She asked if I wanted to grab lunch. I said I was open to anywhere so long as they took credit cards, as I didn't have any cash. She picked someplace in I think an old depot and we had gyros. As they didn't take credit cards, she paid for me. I would have paid if she had listened to me. Since she almost got me shot, I think she kind of owed me the free lunch. She took me back to my hotel and I was almost late for my shuttle to the airport. I thanked her and sent a message later thanking her for the fun time. I guess she did not have a good time because she did not respond. Oh well, if you somehow are reading this, thanks for the free lunch. Unless of course, you are in heaven looking down after being killed by attempting to break into another national landmark. Then I say I told you so.

#167

Don't Walk 5 Miles With Drunk People

People think after 19 years that I have all these stories about adventures on layovers. Unfortunately, I have very few. This story is by far my craziest. When you add in the fact the other person in it later made national news. It makes it even funnier. The story takes place in Lincoln, Nebraska. Which is funny, because about a year later a flock of geese tried to take me out as well. That story isn't funny though so I will not be sharing it. Needless to say, "Stinkin Lincoln" as some aviation people refer to it does not conjure up fond memories. We arrived at our hotel in the early afternoon. The First Officer decided that we were going to go to downtown Lincoln for lunch. The hotel van dropped us off at a restaurant and said to call when we needed picked up. This was in the era before Uber and Lyft so this story would not take place today. We eat lunch and the FO is ripping on the Captain for showing pictures of his baby and talking about it a lot. He said he was probably back in the hotel talking to his wife on the phone. I don't know how that is an insult but that was his intent when he said it. At the end of the night, I was wishing that I too had stayed in my room. I told him it was cool that he was happy to be a Dad. After finishing lunch, he asks the waitress where we could play pool. I suck at pool, but I was bored so we headed to the bar she recommended. We get there at 3:55pm. The bartender informs us that pool isn't free until 4pm. There was no one else in the bar so we waited 5 minutes. We start playing pool at 4 and PBRs are $1 at 4. I didn't drink but played pool. This homeless guy comes in and puts down tons of change to get 1 beer. He sat there and made that 1 beer last forever. The FO decides to call his buddy and tell him all about the $1 PBRs and how the next time that he is in Lincoln he needs to check it out. He raved about how awesome the place was. It was a bar with a pool table nothing special. His standard of awesome is a lot lower than mine apparently. I find out later this FO was a party guy and was known as the naked pilot. Apparently, he would get naked anytime he got drunk. We decided we wanted to head back to the hotel. He calls the hotel and finds out they cannot pick us up for another 4 hours at 9pm. We are like uhhhh, no. The bar tells us there really aren't any cabs this time of the day. Since we didn't have the luxury of smartphones, we didn't know how far the distance truly was. We decided to walk back to the hotel. After getting back to the hotel, I MapQuest it and find out we walked 5.5 miles. We start our journey and get a block before FO sees this bar called Hole in the Wall or something close to that. He insists that we have to stop for one drink. I'm like whatever. I forgot to mention it was 96 degrees outside so the stop with AC was ok by me. He gets a beer and asks for a plastic cup for chew. He tries to flirt with the bartender and asks her name. Her name was Raisca or something similar. He keeps messing it up and annoying her. She turns around and he loudly says, "I'd like to hit that up the ass." I am embarrassed and annoyed at his stupidity. She either didn't hear it or ignores him. He finishes his drink, and we head out. A few blocks away he sees this woman approaching. He yells to her, "hey baby, you're the prettiest thing I've seen all day." She ignores him and just as she passes next to him, he blurts out, "Nah, she was ugly." We continue on and he declares he needs to take a piss. He stops and pees on the side of the post office in broad daylight. I think since it is a federal building that makes it a felony. We walk on and he sees the two most uptight looking girls and decides to ask them for a ride to the airport. I think sober they wouldn't given him a ride. They decline and we journey on. Each step I get more and more annoyed at him. We see a short cut that involves cutting through empty lots and crossing railroad tracks. A seemingly endless coal train comes through and after 100+ cars go by it is clear to cross. We stop and a manual train track switching track is pulled. I didn't hear of any derailments so apparently it didn't do anything harmful. We walk by a radio controlled car park and bmx park. He stops to yell at the people at both parks and call them losers. A drunk walking 5 miles in 96 degree heat has no right to call anyone a loser. Thankfully, we approach commercial development and from my guesstimate about 2/3 of the way to the hotel. We stop at a gas station. I get Gatorade as I am about to die of heat stroke, and he gets some smokes. As we are continuing our regional airline version of trek to Mordor, he decides to enlighten me. "Did you know that you can get your dick sucked through a hole in the wall by a hot chick in Wichita for $30." I am shocked at both the timing of that revelation and the fact he shared that with someone he barely knew. I reply, "that was a dude." "No, it wasn't. It was a hot chick", he protests. "Did you see the hot chick sucking it?" "No". "Then it was a dude." He apparently had never pondered this possibility. I don't know the 2005ish rates of sexual favors but $30 seems really low, especially for a hot chick. I don't recall how it ended but the conversation quickly switched to dinner. We decided to stop at Perkins. If you have never been to Perkins, the best comparison would be a midwestern Denny's that's slightly classier. We both get meals that include dinner and dessert. As we wait for the check, I see that our meal was supposed to include rolls which we did not receive. I mention that and he loudly yells, "I want my F'ing rolls!!!" Somehow there are no Perkins employees in the dining room at the time but there are a bunch of families. At this point I am beyond done with this idiot. I inform him that he's eaten his meal and dessert and does not need rolls. As we walk the final two blocks, I vow to myself to never fly with this idiot ever again. I remember walking into the lobby and seeing the jetBlue flight where everyone on the plane was watching themselves on satellite tv as they circled to burn off fuel to make an emergency landing. One of those know it alls who call into CNN was giving his opinion. The anchor kept calling him Captain. He corrected them, "I am only a First Officer". A few years later as my First Officer made the news someone called me and said his name and Captain. I tried to correct them, and they said no he is a Captain. I'll never forget saying, "who made that idiot a Captain." There are a few lessons here. Don't drink too much is an obvious one. Take an uber when necessary. Don't pee on the post office. Don't say offensive things to women. Always make sure there isn't an obstacle shielding you from seeing your partner in intimate moments. The most important one is that a title and increased responsibility doesn't make someone more responsible.

#168

Don't Open Closed Bins

A closed overhead bin is the international sign for a bin being full. It may be full of emergency equipment or luggage from other passengers, but it is full. Please do not open closed bins. You hold up boarding. I understand that you want to put your bag above you. That is not always possible. You may have to put your bags in bins further from you. The space above you is not assigned to you as many passengers have tried to insist. Place luggage that will fit under your seat. Find an open bin for the baggage that is too big to fit under seats. It is not a difficult concept but for some people it seems to be. Rollerbags have priority in overhead bin space. Don't be selfish and put your little bag or jacket in a bin. Some people close bins so that someone else won't put a bag in with theirs. That is selfish and often results in us having to open bins looking for space for the bags of others. Make our job easier and leave it open unless it is actually full. If you have to put your bag a few rows back, don't push your way back to retrieve it while deplaning. Let the few rows behind you deplane. When there are small gaps during deplaning move back a few rows at a time. Then you can retrieve your bag without being rude. There is no need to yell back at the people in the rows by your baggage and ask them to hand it up. Be patient and courteous. Stowing baggage isn't hard, but people seem to make it hard. Most important of all, be careful around other people's bags and don't smash theirs while putting yours in. Boarding and deplaning is a lot smoother for everyone if a little courtesy is used when stowing baggage.

#169

It's Not Your Fight

There is a saying people much younger than me use that refers to staying in your lane. I'm not young and hip so I may be misinterpreting this, but my understanding is that it means don't get involved in things you know nothing or very little about or don't involve you. It seems like now days everyone is looking to be part of a fight. They will jump in on topics they haven't been involved in or do not have firsthand details about. I believe in supporting friends in disagreements but make sure you have the facts before you go crazy. Just like the news, everyone wants to be the first one on the scene. No one wants to take a step back and look at the whole situation and all the facts before reacting. Analyze then react. It will save unnecessary escalations and taking sides you might not take if you knew all the facts. Leave the fighting to those actually involved.

#170

Don't Be A Karen

Everyone knows what a Karen is. I've had to deal with them long before we had a name for them. I created a system mentally on who could be a potential problem. I want to be clear that not everyone who fits the criteria has been a problem. In fact, the number of problems I've experienced over the years have been relatively few. That may be because I am male or because as someone once said I look mean. The problems, which have been small in number, have almost always been because of someone who fit the mental criteria I made up. Once I told a coworker about my system. Later in the flight, she said someone was giving her a hard time. I asked if she remembered who I said would be a problem. She recited what I had said and then said, "omg, you're right." Karens usually make me laugh when they rant at gate agents expecting it to work. One Karen insisted she be rebooked on another airline. They tried to explain that she would arrive later than our delayed flight, but she didn't care. My favorite moment was one flight when we were sitting waiting to take off. I could see from my jumpseat, that a plane that had just landed had their landing gear collapse. The Captain made an announcement saying that we would be standing by until we were told what to do. This Karen sitting next to my jumpseat was angry and said, "how long do these things usually take anyways?" I said, "In 15 years of flying, I have never had a plane have its landing gear collapse in front of me, so I have no idea." That didn't satisfy her so I said, "well it is a private plane so it will take a lot less time than a commercial flight would." That was a pure Karen moment. Don't be a Karen. It's not hard, be patient and kind. If you can't be either of those be quiet. It is possible, and I believe in you.

#171

Have Your Order Ready

I try to serve passengers as quickly as possible. There are a variety of reasons for that. One is that by being in the aisle, I am blocking access to one of our two restrooms and on one plane type, the only restroom. One of the other reasons is that I am the only one not in a seatbelt. If we encounter clear air turbulence, which cannot be predicted, I am the most at risk of injury. The occurrence of turbulence has risen greatly in the past few years. I have personally witnessed a Flight Attendant get injured. You can help us avoid being injured and help your fellow passengers get to the restroom sooner. The way you can do that is by having your tray table down and your order ready. This will help the process go quickly and smoothly. I know the choice of beverages differs by airline, but we all have the same basic choices. Cola, Diet Cola, Lemon Lime, Ginger Ale, Juices, Coffee and Water are available for you. The snack options are the biggest difference. You can usually see what is being given out to rows ahead of you or you can overhear what is being offered to them. Some airlines have their choices available on their website. In the past you could read the inflight magazine in the seat pocket, but I believe almost all airlines have eliminated those. It is a small gesture having your order ready, but we appreciate it. It makes our job easier and safer. So, remember to know what you want and have your tray table down. If you say please we would love that too, but we will settle for the other two requests.

#172

Poop In The Back Of The Plane

I understand at times the nearest restroom needs to be utilized. However, when time permits, please poop in the back restroom of the plane. In the front of the plane, the smell seems to linger and waft up to the flight deck. The pilots usually call back and make some sarcastic comment asking if we are feeling ok or need to change our diaper. First class is usually stuck smelling it. First-Class passengers will make comments and ask if we have some sort of air freshener. Unfortunately, the air freshener that they provide us with makes it smell like chemical covered poop. Much like when people who haven't showered, think that they can cover up their body odor by baptizing themselves in cologne. Not the Catholic sprinkle but the Baptist full immersion. The end result is usually worse than better. First Class will often have a meal during their flight. They will have to try and eat with the horrible smell. Not to mention, the First-Class flight attendant is stuck smelling it while trying to prepare and serve drinks and snacks. It's just a simple request. Both passengers and crew have committed this offense, so this request is directed at both types of flyers. We just ask that when it is possible, use the back restroom. When you make that choice. Everyone's nose will thank you.

#173

Be Ready At Security

Security at the airport can take forever. On busy days in big cities, it can last several hours. A big reason for that are people that are unprepared. Their liquids are not in one bag. They are not the correct size bottles. Electronics are not removed from bags before being sent through the x-ray machine. People also have phones and metal in their pockets when they go through the medical detector. If you don't fly often, I suggest visiting the TSA's website before traveling. It will give you the most up to date information on what you can and can't bring. You can also familiarize yourself with the procedures you will be going through. It can help make your security experience less stressful and save you time. I suggest making a mental plan for when you get to the security line. I always remove anything from my pockets while waiting in line. I have a plan for the order of how I put my things on the x-ray belt. I put my smaller bag in the first bin. Then I put my suitcase. The next bin is where I put my laptop after I remove it from my suitcase. The last bin is where I put my shoes. By the time my shoes have come out of the x-ray machine, my laptop is back in my suitcase and my smaller bag is on top of my suitcase. I can grab my shoes and either slip them on right there or walk over to a bench and put them on. It is fast, efficient and most important of all. I am not holding up the line. If more people had a plan. The line would move a lot quicker for everyone. Save time and plan ahead.

#174

Keep Your Ignorant Comments To Yourself

Airline crew are always thrown under the bus by gate agents. If something is delayed for crew reasons, they always make it seem like we are the problem. When in reality, our appearance at the gate is usually not by our choice, nor is the delay our fault. We are usually reassigned to cover for someone else who cannot work their flight for whatever reason. They could have called in sick. They could be stuck in another city because their plane is delayed for maintenance, atc or weather. The rules have changed but previously we could be reduced to 8 hours of rest. There has always been this misconception that means 8 hours of sleep. Our rest starts 15 minutes after our flight arrives. A lot of times, that is when we are walking off the plane after deplaning. At a lot of airports, we are getting in the van 10 minutes later and then a 10-minute van ride to the hotel. That puts us at 7 hours and 40 minutes of rest. Let's say we are lucky, and a fast-food place is next door. We get dinner and quickly eat it. That takes 40 minutes. Now we are at 7 hours of rest. Since we are in the air all day, we may have calls or emails to make. Let's say that takes 30 minutes and includes getting ready for bed. Now we are at 6 hours and 30 minutes. We get up an hour before our van time, so we are now at 5 hours and 30 minutes of rest. Best case scenario, the hotel is close and does a shuttle on demand and not top and bottom of every hour like a lot of hotels. We have to factor in time for security, so our total sleep opportunity was 5 hours. Now because of a change in rules, we can be reduced to 10 hours which gives us a chance at 7 hours of sleep in the best-case scenario. It is much better, but still not a lot of sleep. Occasionally, for whatever reason, we arrive late the night before. They have to adjust our rest to allow for the minimum time. That means in the morning our flight is delayed. It's delayed so that we can get around 7 hours of sleep which is not a ton of sleep. When flights are delayed for crew rest, gate agents always make sure to tell that to the passengers. The passengers have no idea that we are only getting a small amount of sleep and will sometimes make angry comments as the crew arrives at the gate. I will never forget this angry old woman in Des Moines, Iowa. As we walked by, she said, "I hope you enjoyed your sleep." We were only delayed around 10 minutes. I only had around 5 hours of sleep and was certainly not as well rested as she thought. I whipped my head around to look at her. She looked shocked and did not say a word. I know someone who once was assigned a very delayed flight. The passengers were all angry and made comments to the crew as they approached the gate. They knew that they needed to take control of the situation. They loudly said that anyone who made comments to the crew as they boarded were not taking the flight. They informed the gate agent that the delay was not their fault. They informed them that if passengers were hostile to the crew. No one was going to their destination. They said the first person who came on was an elderly woman who looked at them, shook her head and didn't say a word. They said everyone else was very friendly and the flight was actually very pleasant. They said they didn't know if their comments helped, but they were glad the flight went so smoothly. A friend recently was reassigned to work a flight. The flight was delayed when they arrived at the gate. As passengers boarded, one of them told my friend that the gate agent had made an announcement. The agent said that my friend was late for work and blamed him for the delay. As they stood to do the safety demo, this passenger decided to make a joke about him being the one who was late for work. My friend informed them that he was the one who was supposed to be headed to his layover and instead was made to work this flight. He stated that the delay was not due to him, but that he was there to get them to their destination. The passenger was suddenly apologetic and was glad that my friend was there. My friend said, "you don't need to be sorry, as you bought a ticket with the expectation to get to your destination. People just need to know the facts". The next time your flight is delayed, before you say something to the crew, remember that it might not be their fault.

#175

Heroes Are Human

The internet has ruined my childhood. You learn more and more about your heroes who are just terrible humans. If you grew up in Minnesota during the late 80s and early 90s, your hero was Kirby Puckett. He was the posterchild for people who have worked hard to overcome the odds. Physically, he did not have the body of an athlete. He was small and chubby, but he worked his butt off to make it to the major leagues. Through his hard work, he had a hall of fame career. He was beloved in Minnesota by anyone who was a Twins fan. Old people, young people, people of all races, we all loved Kirby. It was after his career was cut short from glaucoma, that we learned about the real Kirby. He had domestic violence issues with his wife. He had allegedly tried to saw through the bathroom door when his wife locked herself in there to get away from him. He had a long-term mistress who said he would pee in a parking lot at a mall. He said that he was Kirby Puckett, and he could do anything in Minnesota. He also allegedly tried to rape a woman at a restaurant. He was not the man we all loved. Actually, he was the man we all loved but we didn't know who we were loving. He died rather young after battling health issues. He died a man no longer the hero, but one many regretted for idolizing. Humans are just that human. They do not deserve to be put on pedestals because they will all fall. It may not be a scandalous fall, but they will never live up to the high level you have placed them at. It is popular now to have celebrity pastors who people follow religiously. Everyone is at risk to fall, even if they are a religious leader. I remember as a young college student this pastor who was the "cool" pastor. He was in his early 50s and related really well to younger people. I was disappointed to learn that he had an affair after I had moved away. There are countless stories of celebrities in different fields making mistakes and not living up to the image people have of them. Some are even esteemed and thought to be of high moral character. Admire people, but realize that they are also human and prone to make mistakes like you and me.

#176

Act Without Regret

While I am not a pilot, I have always been a fan of airplanes. Everyone who loves planes love the 747. That's a given. One of the coolest planes ever flown was the Concorde. It flew at twice the speed of sound and went from New York to London in under 4 hours. It was very expensive and seen as only for the rich. In early 2003, both British Airways and Air France announced that they were retiring their Concordes by the end of the year. The Concorde had gotten to be too expensive to fly. I was a young 21-year-old who had always wanted to fly on it. It so happened, that they announced the retirement of the Concorde right before my 22nd birthday. Tickets were $4,000 for one way on the Concorde and back in coach on a 747. Common sense says that $4,000 is too much money to spend, just to ride on an airplane. Common sense lost out to my Visa card. I didn't want to live with the regret of not being able to fly twice the speed of sound, at an altitude higher than normal planes fly. You can always make more money, but you can never create more time or experience things that no longer exist. I booked my ticket on British Airways from New York to London. It was going to be an awesome trip. However, the airline I flew on from Minneapolis to New York tried their best to make sure it was not awesome. I had to connect in Detroit and run from one end of the A concourse to the other. I barely made the flight. As I settled in my seat, I wondered if my suitcase had made it. I thought to myself, what a silly thought, of course it made it. It did not make it. I checked into my hotel in New York with just a backpack and no change of clean clothes. I had somehow cut my knuckle on the way to the airport and had a patch of blood the size of an orange on my jeans. I had to use the hotel free razor and ketchup pack size of shaving cream. My neck looked like I had been stabbed in 1000 places. I had to buy deodorant and a t shirt at the airport. I was allergic to the deodorant, so my arm pits burned. I checked in for the flight, with just a small backpack. I was surprised that I didn't have to go through extra security screening. A guy with blood-stained clothes and almost no luggage, flying on an expensive plane, should have raised some red flags or so I thought. It was still an amazing experience that I will never forget. The service and food were awesome. After the flight, I got to visit the flight deck and look around. It was something I would have regretted forever if I hadn't done it. I am so glad common sense lost the day I booked my ticket. There is something I am sure you have always wanted to do. Do it without regret.

#177

Do What You Promise

We often make promises and later regret making them. We hope the person we made the promise to forgets or we make excuses why we cannot fulfill the promise. We as a society need to stop that. We need to leave the empty promises to politicians. Once, I promised a friend of a friend that I would let him tag along with me to London the next time I went. After I got to know him, I really did not want to keep that promise. I was hoping that he would forget. The next time I planned a trip to London, I let him know I was going. I asked if he would like to come along. I was hoping that he would say no. Unfortunately for me, he was happy to join my father and I. I spent the next few weeks dreading our trip. I had created an itinerary that allowed for some free time. Of course, several of the days he chose to tag along, instead of going out on his own. After the week was over, he was very appreciative of me allowing him to come along. I felt bad for being grumpy that he had come with me. I realized two things that day. How important it is to keep your promises, no matter how uncomfortable it makes you. I also realized that one should make as few promises as possible. I have been more careful since then and have given vague responses before promising things. However, once I've made a promise, I have honored it. Always do what you say, no matter how much it hurts.

#178

Be Careful With The Plane

The structure of airplanes and its moving parts are fairly sturdy. The interiors of them are often not. One of the most broken items are overhead bins. They are made of plastic. When people force luggage in them that doesn't fit and try to close them, they break. It doesn't happen too often thankfully. However, when it happens, we have to empty that bin and the bin next to it since they are basically one bin with 2 doors on it. Over time, I have learned what to do to speed up the process, before maintenance arrives to tape the bin closed. I empty the bins and move luggage around, so all they have to do is tape it closed, put a do not use sticker on it, and fill out the paperwork. It doesn't save a ton of time, but when people have connecting flights to make, every minute helps. On a funny side note, no matter how many stickers and tape are on it saying it isn't usable. There are always passengers who try and open it. It is funny until they succeed. Then we have to call maintenance out to retape it closed. One time, a broken bin resulted in a quite amusing situation. It was the last flight of the night from Cincinnati to New York. The flight was delayed due to storms in New York. The pilots were nearing the time where they would time out and be unable to operate any more flights that day. We boarded up and were about ready to go. This gentleman in 3A tried to jam his bag in an overhead bin and broke the bin. For some reason, the bin I have experienced being broken the most is over 1C/D. I informed the Captain. He made a PA stating that a bin was broken and that we would have to wait for maintenance. The gentleman who broke the bin rang his call light, and I could tell he was angry. He started to yell at me. He said that we shouldn't have boarded people onto a broken plane. As he was the reason the plane was broken, I felt it necessary to inform him why the plane was broken. I said firmly but politely that the aircraft was not broken until he broke it. It was his bag that broke the bin and caused us to have to call maintenance. He suddenly got really quiet. After maintenance came out, we found out that we missed our takeoff time, and our flight was canceled. The gate agent came onboard to inform the passengers and tell them that due to the act of God clause in tickets. The airline would not be providing them hotel rooms. The guy who broke the bin was in 3A, but somehow was the first person off the plane. He was moving pretty fast deplaning. It was either guilt or that he didn't want people to confront him. I have never seen anyone deplane that fast before or since. The lesson here is be kind to the airplane. If your bag doesn't fit, ask for help. It is better to check your bag than break a bin. It might not cancel a flight but if it does. Everyone will know it was because of you.

#179

Don't Be A Diva

I have met several celebrities in my job. Overall, most of them don't want to be recognized or bothered. Some of them understand that is the price of fame and are very kind to fans. I remember sitting in the gate area waiting for our plane to arrive. I heard a voice that I recognized around the corner from me. I knew it but couldn't place it. I walked around the corner and saw that it was a former talk show host. He was just sitting there talking to people like they were old friends. He was posing for pictures. You would have thought he was someone's uncle. He understood the game and was very gracious with his time. I told him when he boarded that it was the other flight attendant's birthday. He wished him Happy Birthday and shook his hand. The majority of other celebrities usually board last or wear a hat. I understand that behavior. You are famous but also human. You don't need to be bothered 100% of the time. I have had a good chat with a hall of fame baseball player. I joked that I shouldn't give him dinner as he had made me sad many times in my childhood by beating the Twins. He laughed and apologized. I know of one particular celebrity story that I will never forget. The Flight Attendant always looked over the passenger list before boarding for names they recognized. They saw one they knew from a show on tv. They were taking predeparture drink orders and got to the celebrity. They ordered a white wine. The Flight Attendant informed them they had just served the last one and apologized. The passenger directly across the aisle had gotten it. The celebrity glared at them and started yelling at the Flight Attendant about how it was unacceptable to be out of white wine before the flight even left. The Flight Attendant again apologized and said that they had communicated the issue to catering but was unsure if the catering truck would arrive before departure. The celebrity said that was not acceptable. They then threatened to tweet about the Flight Attendant. The Flight Attendant after being berated several times for an issue they had not created and had exhausted all solutions to solve was not going to be threatened. They informed the celebrity that the issue was not of their creation, they had done everything in their power to attempt to remedy the problem and that the celebrity was yelling at the wrong

198

person. They then informed the celebrity that if they were going to tweet. They are going after the person who is not at fault for this. The celebrity looked shocked that someone had stood up to them and didn't say a word. The Flight Attendant then asked if they would like something else and they said no. The Flight Attendant checked when they landed, and the celebrity had not tweeted about them. One of my favorite stories was of a reality star on a flight from Nashville to NYC. The Flight Attendant recognized her name on the departure report and from her show. She was cuddling with a gentleman the whole flight in first class. The Flight Attendant had a magazine and there just happened to be an article in it about this woman. It talked about her and her fiancée. The Flight Attendant looked at the picture of her fiancée. It did not appear to be the person she was cuddling with. They leaned out of the galley to look at him again. They were almost certain it was not her fiancée, so they grabbed the departure paperwork to confirm. The person the reality star was traveling and cuddling with was not her fiancée. They laughed to themselves about having celebrity gossip that they couldn't share with anyone. If you're famous or just a diva, please don't be rude. We will give you the best service that we can, but we do not deserve to be mistreated because other people allow you to behave that way.

#180

Depression Is Real

For the majority of my life, I have been nervous around women that I have been attracted to. I am not shy. I just think and worry too much. My wife has told me that I am clueless when women are flirting with me which is true. I don't know if it is being self-conscious or my constant fear of failure, but I have always been worried about how I look or what they will think of me. I become the human version of a computer operating in safe mode. I have less functions and overthink my responses and actions. I have learned over time, that the other person, if they are attracted to me is just as nervous and self-conscious as I am. The person who I worried was in this position of power emotionally is just as vulnerable as I am. If I had known that I would have taken more chances and dated more. I was so worried about the possible nos; that I didn't take the chance one might be a yes. This led to me having periods of depression in my teen years and early 20s. I attended a Christian college my freshmen year. The number of women who attended outnumbered the men. People joked that many of the women were just there for a Mrs. degree. That made things worse for me. I could not get past my nervousness and that made me more depressed. Humans need a human connection. Even someone like me who tries to reduce their human contact, still needs it from time to time. I was surrounded by people but felt so alone. I had become depressed to the point that I thought about jumping off the bridge by the dam not far from campus. I had a friend in 9th grade who killed themselves. It didn't inspire me, but it made me think about what they were feeling that caused them to go through with it. What made them feel that there was no light at the end of the tunnel? I have always been an overthinker which in some situations has caused me not to do things. The more I thought about something, the less likely I was going to do it, which was a good thing. But the depression still remained. One day I don't remember why, but I was even more depressed than usual. I took a bottle of Tylenol and poured some in my hand. I was going to take it all. At the time, I didn't know if it would work. I just wanted my depression to stop. As I stood there with a handful of Tylenol, someone knocked at my door. They were insistent that I come hang out with them. To this day, they have no idea what their knock stopped from happening. If it would have killed me or not, thankfully I will never know. While many people suffer from mental illness and depression some of us feed our depression. We are blinded by our feelings and allow them to steer our path. Until you are ever dealing with those thoughts and feelings you can never understand. You feel like you are drowning and cannot save yourself. You see the surface but can't get there. It feels like just when you think you are about to break the surface, you sink further down. It can be any issue, not just relationships that can trap you in depression. The problem with a lot of Christians is how we deal with mental health. People who are depressed are seen as having a lack of faith. They treat people with depression and mental issues as less than or having something wrong with them. You don't pray enough is a common thought. "It's just the devil messing with you." The way of thinking that is prevalent in Christianity today is contrary to what Jesus would do and say. Jesus had compassion and we should as well. Psalm 34:18 says, "The Lord is near to the brokenhearted and saves the crushed in spirit." Seeking help for whatever issues you have is not a lack of faith in God. One thing to remember is that Luke, who was one of the disciples was a doctor. Jesus healed people but still had a doctor as a disciple. I am no theologian but to me that is significant. Why would He have someone with Him if He were opposed to the medical profession? Christians need to embrace the mental health profession and support those who are seeking help. If you are struggling with depression no matter your religious beliefs, please seek help. You are not alone. It may feel like whatever you are going through is more than you can handle. We are limited in what we can do alone, but with others we can carry a much bigger burden. You are not the first person to go through what you are going through. Others who have gone down the same road can help share what they have overcome. They can help you on the road to healing. Don't be afraid. You can overcome. I thought long and hard about sharing my own experiences. People can use our experiences against us or try and paint us as weak. I realized that even if it could possibly help one person it was worth the risk of possible embarrassment.

#181

Jesus Ain't Your Cash Machine

Even if you haven't been involved with Christianity, you at least know the jokes about the televangelists asking for money. Many of them are a part of what is called prosperity gospel. It is the belief that if you give money to the church, then God will "bless" you. By bless, they imply you will get rich. The preachers in the prosperity gospel movement often are in expensive suits, drive luxury cars and live in huge houses. They are nothing more than charlatans and hustlers looking to prey on the desperate and poor. I believe God does bless people but nowhere in the Bible does it say that He will make you rich. I had the unfortunate displeasure of attending a college that subscribed to that belief for one year. They would bring in all these famous preachers who would preach about what God would do for you if you had faith. The common phrase is sowing your seed in faith to reap a harvest. They all use some variation of that phrase. One preacher had us all yell, "money cometh unto me, NOW!!!" We had to pretend like we were flushing a toilet or something so the blessings would come. They always have about 2–3-hour services. You sing songs and then you have the offering sermon. The offering sermon usually takes about 30 to 45 minutes. It is basically an infomercial on how God has blessed the preacher or someone they know. One preacher would talk about how he blessed someone and now he never has to pay to eat at Popeyes. Then they take the offering after which the main sermon begins. The main sermon is like an hour long. One of these conmen bragged about how he has the biggest house in his state because he is blessed. Even if you do not belief in the divinity of Christ, you will see this type of thinking is contrary to what Jesus said to do. He said to help the poor and the widows. He didn't say anything about making anyone rich. One time in my life, I was very low on money. The hotel did not have free breakfast and I was very hungry. At the airport I was flying out of, you have to walk through the duty-free store. This employee ambushed me to try some cookies. She insisted that I take several of them. I have been through that airport tons of times. Never before that day or since has anyone offered free cookies. While it is not a new BMW, it was a blessing, and I was thankful.

Jesus isn't a genie who will grant your financial wishes. The offering is not an investment fund or lottery ticket. If you give, do it for the sake of giving and not with the expectation of receiving anything. Jesus said it is better to give than receive. If you are one of these preachers, you will be judged for misleading people for financial gain. Repent and use your platform to do as the Bible commands us to. Christians need to think less about what God can do for them and more about what they can do for God.

#182

Sit By The Wings

People always ask me where the safest place to sit is on the airplane. Depending upon what happens, there may be no seat that is safe. If the plane isn't breaking up before impact, a lot of times the majority of the fuselage remains intact. The tail up to the wings a lot of times is what survives. I am going by what I have been told. I am neither a pilot nor an aerospace engineer so if I am incorrect in what, I say I apologize. I have been told that the area by the wings is the strongest part of the plane structurally, because it has to hold the wings onto the plane and absorb all the forces the wings experience. I usually sit by the wings for a few reasons. The first being because I was told that is the strongest part of the plane. The second being that I am close to an exit if we need to evacuate. That is also why I choose an aisle seat. No one wants to not be able to get out, if the aisle seat person freezes up or is worried about their luggage during the evacuation. It is also a smoother ride if the aircraft has wing mounted engines. The rows behind the engines allegedly have a bumpier ride. I have noticed that several times. There are only a handful of planes with engines mounted to the fuselage. In that case, your ride allegedly shouldn't be that much different behind the wings. Everyone has their favorite place on the aircraft to sit for different reasons. Sit wherever you feel most comfortable but always make sure you know your potential evacuation route. I sit where I feel the safest and most comfortable. You should do the same.

#183

Don't Buckle Up Just Yet

This one is a little annoyance and a little superstition. If you are in the aisle seat and one or more seats next to you are empty, do not buckle up. It seems like people hurry to board and buckle as soon as they sit down. If you're the first person to board of the 150 sitting in the gate area. The odds are good that you will have a seatmate. They always get annoyed when someone comes to sit in their row, and they have to unbuckle. They act like it is this huge inconvenience when conventional wisdom would tell them to wait to buckle. Humans are sometimes superstitious or do things for certain reasons. I never buckle up when I am in the aisle seat until the aircraft door closes if there are empty seats in my row. I believe if I buckle up prematurely, then someone will come to occupy the empty seat. If I am not seated in the aisle seat, I inform the aisle seatmate of my beliefs and urge them not to jinx us. If someone comes to sit in our row. I joke that it's because they buckled up. There is no scientific data to support my belief, but I remain unbuckled just to be safe. If you're in the aisle and have empty seats just wait to buckle. It might help a silly superstition come true or just keep you from being annoyed from having to unbuckle.

#184

Don't Cut In Line

From preschool on, in life you will have to deal with line cutters. It is one of the most annoying things. You did your time waiting and this fool thinks that they can sneak into the line. Many a fight has ensued because of line cutters. Airports are full of lines, from security to the food court, to the bathrooms and boarding. For the most part, people don't try and cut lines. Usually, the boarding line is attempting to be semi organized chaos. You usually do have the gate lice infesting the area. You have to make like an NFL running back trying to find a hole to get to the door to board. Sometimes people do wait on the side of the crowd and sneak into line. That inconveniences you for like 7 seconds. You can't always blame them for not always knowing who is trying to board when there are people standing everywhere. I did have a funny experience with a line cutter one time at security. I was based at an airport where I rode a train to the terminal. This person worked for a competing airline. He got off the train and cut me off to get on the escalator. Then when we got to the security line, he cut me off again. I was seriously annoyed but not wanting to create a scene. I stayed quiet. A few weeks later, I was watching the news. There was a story about an incident where a Flight Attendant was arrested for committing a crime. They show his picture and I blurt out, "Omg, he's the guy who cut ahead of me in the security line." Being the occasionally petty person, I had a really good laugh at his expense. I guess after there are worse things than cutting in line but maybe that was his gateway to getting arrested. Cutting lines today, committing crimes tomorrow. I shouldn't have to say this but don't cut in line.

#185

Be Kind

I have shared some things that I have learned in life and in my job. Some may have made you laugh and some you may not agree with. The one thing that I have learned in life is that everyone has something going on you cannot see. It's like a car with a fancy paint job but under the hood there are issues. Some people are fighting something, and a kind word or gesture may push them to carry on. The inverse of that, is they might be ready to give up and a harsh word or gesture may cause them to do that. We never can fully know the impact of what we say or do. There are people that I had no clue that I had impacted, thank me for things that I have said or done. I have had people that I don't really even know that well ask why I don't like them. When in reality, I do not have a bad opinion about them. When a plane crashes, it doesn't matter what you look like, who you love, how much money you have or how you vote. What happens on the plane happens to everyone. There are people who I can tell don't agree with me on some issues because of their shirt or button on their luggage. I treat them with the same respect as people I agree with. We need to get back to being a world where we can agree to disagree. It is ok to think differently. Our enemy is not each other but the mindset that thinking differently means we are enemies. I urge you in your travels and in life to talk to the people who are different than you. You may not become friends, but you are both working to bring the world together and not divide it. We are all passengers on Earth. We only get one trip on it. Let's make it one that leaves it a better place than when we boarded.

About the Author

If sarcasm was a language, Timo would be considered fluent. Sarcasm and humor have kept him sane in 19 years as a Flight Attendant. He loves to laugh and to make people laugh. He can usually be found downing gallons of the nectar of the gods, Dr. Pepper. You can reach him by email timodavidbooks@gmail.com